3o

Things Everyone
Should Know How to Do
Before Turning 3o

3<u>0</u>
Things Everyone Should Know How to Do Before Turning 30

by Siobhan Adcock

pictures by
Patrick Mortensen

Broadway Books / New York

PRINTED IN THE UNITED STATES OF AMERICA

BROADWAY BOOKS and its logo, a letter B bisected on the diagonal,
are trademarks of Random House, Inc.

Visit our website at www.broadwaybooks.com

First edition published 2003

Book design by Laurie Jewell
Illustrated by Patrick Mortensen

Library of Congress Cataloging-in-Publication Data

Adcock, Siobhan.
   30 things everyone should know how to do before turning 30 /
by Siobhan Adcock ; pictures by Patrick Mortensen.
      p. cm.
   1. Success.   2. Life skills.   3. Conduct of life.   I. Title: Thirty things
everyone should know how to do before turning thirty.   II. Title.
BJ1611.2 .A26 2003
646.7—dc21

                                 2002038242

ISBN 0-7679-1397-3

10 9 8 7 6 5 4 3 2 1

Acknowledgments

The smartest thing anybody can do is to surround herself with brilliant friends.

Thanks to:
Mom and Gilly, Andrew Roth, Andrew Corbin, Patrick the Invincible, Becky Cole, Jim Rutman, Gerry Howard, Megan Ptacek, Janelle Asplund, Melanie Lefkowitz, Tony Shortway, Jen Griffin, Tracy Tuenge, Jason Warner, Chip Harlan, James Caldwell, Andrew Barber, Sharlene Frank, Laura Garrity, Anasuya Sanyal, Anne Leonard, Amanda Touchton, Sarah Lefton, Jenn Chen, Gillian Robertson, Erika Faust, and Sheila O'Malley. You all helped, whether you know it or not. Some of you may be annoyed to discover just how much.

Contents

—

Skills That Save Your Butt, or Someone Else's

How to . . .

Skills That Make You (Feel) Cooler

How to . . .

Skills That Your Grandparents Had That You Should Have Too

How to . . .

Skills That Make the World a Better, More Harmonious and Decent Place

How to . . .

Introduction

People like people who know how to do stuff. It's pretty simple. The secret to making friends and influencing people (and, by the way, to having a nice life) is knowing how to do stuff. This principle actually works on a scale. That is, knowing how to do one or two things really well makes you an interesting, capable person, but knowing how to do, oh, say, thirty things really well makes you, not to put too fine a point on it, kind of extraordinary. Acquiring the skills in this book will make you not just competent, but a guru in a world of mere "go-to" people, a master in an age of dilettantes. Your life will change. You will feel cooler. You will be cooler. Your friends will like you more. Your relatives will love you more. You will go to more parties and at them, you will meet and talk to better-looking people and they will like and respect you. Yes. You. If you're like me or my friends, you probably already know how to do at least a few of these things, but many more are still mysteries to you. The exact reason *why* you don't know this stuff isn't important—there's no need to point fingers at our parents, teachers, or older siblings. We're just correcting for some gaps in our practical education.

Because on a practical, serious level, most of the skills this book has to teach are ones a well-rounded, fully formed person should have mastered by the time she or he is old enough to own property or have kids—and for many people nowadays, that's around the age of thirty. As you approach thirty, you expect to start feeling like a grown-up, or at least more like a grown-up than you did at twenty. The years leading up to your thirties require you to develop a whole new skill set—you're moving ahead in your career, your friends are getting married and having children, your parents and grandparents are getting older, your standard of living is changing. Suddenly you need to know how to spend discretionary income, how to keep house, how to be a good human being (and a good wedding guest), how to maintain a car and an apartment and a career and healthy relationships with your friends and family. All this is part of feeling like a grown-up, but why stop there? The life skills in this book will help you feel not just like a grown-up, but like a badass.

Thirty certainly shouldn't be considered a cutoff point for finding this book useful—it's never too late to learn how to jump start a car. If you're forty-five and surrounded by dead plants and haven't gotten a raise in ten years, there's still something here for you, my friend. This book isn't intended to serve as a long list of ways in which you are inadequate and ill-equipped to face the world. Unless you have really bossy friends (like myself) or know a particularly avuncular repairman, you couldn't possibly have picked up all of this stuff already. You've been too busy dealing with your job and your 401(k) and your vitamin intake. So think of this book as a survival manual for the second most bafflingly ignorant period of your life, your twenties and early thirties (the most bafflingly ignorant period being, naturally, your teens). Read it and go forth with dignity, or at least without making any tremendously embarrassing or expensive mistakes. Unlike the skills and arts taught by so many other arch, glib, "how-to" books and guides, you don't have to buy into a lifestyle or an aesthetic to find this stuff useful. There's no "go-girling" here, no snapping up, no pandering, no artificially enhanced behavioral code of ethics. These are just skills that improve you, and improve the world. Be gallant. Be gracious. Be smart. Be a hero. Be irresistible.

Be an insufferable know-it-all.

30

Things Everyone Should Know How to Do Before Turning 30

Skills That
Save Time or Money

1.

How to Wrap a Present

Why You Should Learn This

A great present wrapped badly or not wrapped at all is a great present, yes. But the person who gets it is still going to think, somewhere deep inside, that despite your wonderful present—which took you months of searching, saving, and covert intelligence-gathering—you didn't really care.

Why do human beings like getting and giving presents? On the receiving end, we like gifts because we're acquisitive little monsters: We like beautiful things, and we especially like ripping beautiful things open. On the other hand, we're also approbation-seeking little ferrets, and we like being responsible for the happiness of other ferrets, in part because that means the other ferrets have to be nice to us. The point is this: Gifts were invented to inspire as much pleasure as possible, on both sides of the transaction. If you skimp on the presentation, you deny the recipient some of the ineffable pleasure of receiving a gift, however much they may claim they don't care that the thing looks like someone juggled it. And in handing a rumpled treasure to someone and expecting them to make the best of it, you rob yourself of the pleasure to be found in doing something really well—well enough to drop jaws, mist eyes, illuminate faces.

And even if you didn't care enough to get a decent present, it should still at least look good so the recipient has *something* nice to say about it. If you're going to give a gift at all, do it right.

How To

First, it's time to set the record straight about some common present-wrapping methods that are in fact kind of lame:

• Presents tucked into mini–shopping bags with tissue paper. We've all done it, but let's admit the truth: It's just flat-out lazy. And even if nesting something in a wad of tissue and dropping it into a bag was the remotest bit difficult or thoughtful, the real crime is that there's no upside for the recipient at all: There's no satisfying paper tearing involved (which is the reason why presents are wrapped to begin with), and what's the recipient supposed to do afterward with a goddamn mini–shopping bag?

• In general, try to avoid giving a present in anything that can't be ripped open and immediately discarded—like paper—or immediately reused, like a cool lunchbox or carrying case, a utile/nifty/nonseasonal storage container, or an attractive cloth bag (like a wine bottle satchel).

• Never aggrandize a small present by putting it in a big box. It is the cruelest joke, as you well know if you have ever been six years old.

• Bows and ribbons are only worth the effort if they actually look good. If you're going to put a bow or ribbon on, make sure it coordinates somehow with the paper, is tied nicely, and doesn't look flimsier or lower quality than the paper itself.

Classic Present-Wrapping Technique

For this you'll need a present in a box, wrapping paper (or tissue paper, or the funnies, or a map, or a clean brown paper bag with the bottom cut off, or a bus schedule, or a roll of uncut counterfeit money, or whatever strikes your little old fancy), a pair of scissors, and a roll of transparent tape. And some practice.

1. Lay out a section or sheet of wrapping paper, decorative side down, on a flat, hard, clean surface. For the purposes of the directions that follow, the top of the paper is "north."

2. Put the box upside down in the center of the paper.

3. Measure and cut the right width (east-west) of paper around the box: Roll out enough paper to wrap around the present and overlap by one finger's width. If you're working with wrapping paper sheets that aren't wide enough, you can tape two sheets together neatly: Fold the western edge of the first sheet one inch under, and fold the eastern edge of the second sheet over one-half inch. Slide the folded section of the second sheet into the folded section of the first sheet and tape the sheets together on the inside.

4. Measure and cut the right length (north-south) of paper: If you've ever wrapped a present before you know this is a hard, but important, measurement to make. If the paper's too long you'll have unwieldy end flaps to deal with, and if the paper's too short you'll end up taping little strips of wrapping paper over the inches of exposed box and hoping no one will notice. Here's a basic rule for cutting wrapping paper for end flaps: When you fold the end of the paper up, it should cover two-thirds of the height of the box.

To conserve paper and cutting time (and have a nice clean edge), scooch the box north on the wrapping paper until the top of the paper is two-thirds the box's height away from the box. Now measure with your fingers (or a ruler, if you're like that) the distance between the north edge of the sheet and the corner of the box, and cut the wrapping paper south of the box to that same length.

5. Pull the east edge of the wrapping paper around the box and tape it to the bottom.

6. Roll the box westward on the paper, using your hands to keep the paper nice and tight around the box. When you've rolled the box completely across, pull the west edge of the paper as tight as you can and tape it down.

7. Now for the ends. Be brave. See how each end has a few inches of paper sticking out on the top, left, right, and bottom? Let's call those top, left, right, and bottom.

8. Top first:

- Pinch the part of top where the paper overlaps, and fold the paper down over the end of the box.

- Use your thumb to make a crease along the top corner of the box.

- If you cut the right length of paper, top should cover two-thirds of the box end. Tape top to the end of the box.

9. Now for left and right:

- You'll see that you've already made triangular bends in left and right. Pinch your fingers along those folds to make good solid creases.

- Fold right inward and use a smidgen of tape to attach it to top.

- Do the same for left.

10. And finally, bottom.

- You'll see you've now made a triangle or trapezoid out of bottom. Fold the end up to create a neat, clean edge, and crease the sides as well.

• Pulling the paper as tight as you can around the box, tape the edge of bottom to top.

11. Repeat on the other end, and you're golden. Some people find it easiest to stand the box on its newly wrapped end while folding the other end. That way you can pull the paper tightly and have a good direct look down at the box end you're working on.

Bows

The two most desirable qualities in a bow are attractiveness and easiness. Adhesive bows are easy but often unattractive. Curling ribbon bows can be both easy and attractive, but in the wrong hands—and those are legion—they can be neither. Cloth ribbons are easy and attractive, and therefore make simple, elegant bows. Here are some basic forms of manipulation:

The Simple Ribbon Bow

1. Cut a length of ribbon that's twice as long as the length of the box, plus three times as wide as the width of the box.

2. Lay the ribbon across the table, and lay the box upside down over it so that the midpoint of the ribbon is right underneath the center of the box top.

3. Pull both ends of the ribbon around the box.

4. Imagine the box is a rectangular clock face: See how the ribbon now reads quarter to three? Holding the ends of the ribbon, rotate the "watch hands" back so that the time is six o'clock.

5. Flip the box over (you can use your thumbs to pin the ribbon ends against the box sides while doing so), and tie a knot with the ribbon. This is your basic baker's knot (à la the string tied around a cake box at a bakery).

6. Tie a regular bow over the baker's knot and snip the ribbon edges so they look neat—for a final touch, you can either cut both ends at an angle or make two diagonal cuts to create a kind of arrow-tail.

The Curling Ribbon Bow

You'll need curling ribbon for this, obviously—don't try it with yarn or cloth—and your scissors.

1. Follow steps 1 through 5 for the simple ribbon bow, above. If you pride yourself on your manual dexterity, you can tie a baker's knot around the present using two or three ribbons at once rather than just one—white tissue paper with three different brightly colored lengths of curling ribbon tied around it can be nice.

2. At the base of one ribbon, close to the baker's knot, pinch the ribbon between your left thumb and index finger.

3. Just above your left thumb, pinch the ribbon between your right thumb and the blade of an open pair of scissors.

4. With a long, steady, upward jerk, slide the scissors blade up the length of the ribbon, holding the ribbon at the base to provide resistance and keep it from twisting. This should produce a highly satisfying *zzzrrrrrrrt* noise.

5. Repeat with the other ribbon(s).

6. If you're not very good at the whole *zzzrrrrrrrt* thing yet, you may find that your curlicues look a bit limp and lame. You can create a perkier effect by adding more curlicues: Cut a few shorter lengths of ribbon, and tie them in a sim-

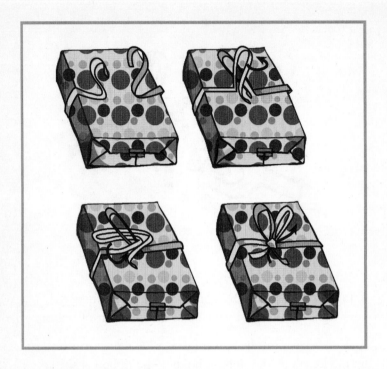

ple knot around the first ribbon knot. Then curl the additional ribbon ends.

The Fancy Bow

This works best with wide cloth or polyester ribbons—the expensive kind. That's why we call it fancy.

1. Follow steps 1 through 4 of the simple ribbon bow.

2. Flip the box over and bring your two ribbon ends back to the top center of the box—but don't tie them in a knot. Instead, create two equal-sized, loose loops that will hereafter be referred to as bunny ears, whether or not it makes this process easier to describe.

3. Pinch the left and right bunny ears at their bases with your fingers, and pull until the ribbon is taut around the box.

4. Still pinching, make a bunny-ear X by crossing the base of the left bunny ear over the base of the right bunny ear. The right bunny ear does not move from this point forward; all the action takes place with the frisky left bunny ear.

5. With your right thumb and index finger, pinch the bases of the two bunny ears together.

6. Now the left bunny ear goes on a trip: It hippety hops in a circle around the right bunny ear.

7. When the left bunny ear gets all the way around, bend the bunny ear down over your right thumb.

8. Now you should see that you've made a loop around the right bunny ear with the base of the left bunny ear, and your thumb is inside that loop. Lift your right thumb and pull the top of the left bunny ear under and up through the loop.

9. Pull the tops of the bunny ears until the knot is tight, then tug the ends to adjust the size of the bow.

10. Finish by cutting both ribbon ends at an angle or cutting two arrow-tails.

Nontraditional Present Wrapping

There are some presents that defy boxes and seem impossible to wrap: shovels, basketballs, turtles. That's when you pull out the heavy artillery.

• Big bright bows. These always get the point across: "I gave you a huge impossible-to-wrap present, or one with legs." Works best with major appliances and cars.

• Winding wrapping paper around every inch. This need not be done particularly neatly, because it also sends a clear message: "I am unable to find a box for this, but I know humans like to shred things with their hands." The effect is time-consuming but amusing, and like most time-consuming but amusing things (evolution, for instance), worth the effort.

• Hiding an unwrapped present and making the recipient hunt for it, or leading the recipient to it while blindfolded.

This is nervy: The payoff, if all goes well, is huge. If you are in any doubt that your present will be greeted with shrieks of surprise and delight, it might go horribly awry. If you choose to go this route, you had better have a really great present. Like a car. Or a horse. Or a European matchbox republic.

2.

How to Start a Successful Fire in a Fireplace, at a Campsite, and in a Barbecue

Why You Should Learn This

There are many modern reasons to learn this most primitive of skills: The person who cheerfully offers on a chilly afternoon to start a roaring fire, to be enjoyed with a nice bottle of red wine by all, is irresistible. The person who correctly and swiftly builds a campfire for the convenience and/or survival of others is a hero. The person who bravely fires up the barbecue for the imminent consumption of ribs and/or tofu dogs is noble. Get the picture?

When it comes to building a fire, efficiency and safety are the better part of valor. A fire that takes too long to build, or sputters out before it can be used or properly snuggled next to, is a waste of time and fuel. Learn to build a good fire, and you earn the respect and gratitude of your fellow men and women.

How to Make a Good Fire in a Fireplace

Do you have chopped firewood? If not, go and find yourself a lumberjack. If you do, then think about laying a fire as an attempt to give your wood the most pleasant burning sensation possible. Ask yourself:

1. Can the wood breathe? Make sure the damper is open so smoke can get up the flue. Know what the flue is? It's a tunnel going up your chimney. Know what the damper is? It's basically a big hatch that closes the flue, so cold air and critters don't get in, and you need to make sure it's open. You can do this by sticking your head into the fireplace and looking up for daylight, or more comfortably, by angling a little mirror into the chimney such that it will reflect any light coming from above. Of course, at night this is a pointless exercise—instead, light a small piece of paper in the chimney. If the smoke goes (mostly) straight up, the damper is open. If it does not, you'll have a mildly smoky room and will need to grope around inside the chimney for the lever or chain that opens the damper. Usually it's on the inside front wall of the fireplace, right on the other side of the brick or stone to which you are pressing your increasingly sooty cheek as you do your groping. Once you find it, pull until you hear a nice solid *thunk*. Your flue is open.

2. Will the wood be grossed out by the fireplace? In order to burn, fire needs oxygen to circulate underneath and around it, so if there's a lot of ash and half-burned wood in the fireplace, you'll need to scoop it out. The little bitty shovel leaning alongside the other fireplace tools may look shiny and eager, but if you've got a lot of ash and big chunks of blackened wood in the hearth, it's not really the best tool for the job. You need something wide, strong, and deep, so get your dustpan. One of those thick, sturdy paper plates will also do—you won't need to clean it, and you can set it on fire later for all its hard work. Scoop the ash toward the back wall and dump (repeatedly) into a garbage bag until your fireplace is clean of debris.

Two caveats: The fireplace doesn't necessarily need to be denuded of all ash—an evenly distributed half inch or so is okay. And if the fireplace has been used in the past week, do not dump the ash into a plastic garbage bag. Use an empty coffee can or aluminum pail instead, since ashes can smolder for days after the fire is out.

3. Does the wood have anything to sit on? Your wood needs to rest above the floor of the fireplace so oxygen can circulate under it and feed your fire. Most fireplaces are equipped with a grate or a pair of andirons, but if yours is not, find some big rocks on which to elevate your wood. Rocks make wood look burly.

4. Are the wood's friends here? Fires cannot live on log alone. Find:

• Paper and/or cardboard. Newspaper is good. Wrapping paper is not good, nor are most gift boxes, because they are laminated with chemicals that often produce mildly toxic fumes, as well as sticky residue that can clog your chimney. Christmas is for recycling, not burning. That said, if you can resist throwing big handfuls of wrapping paper into the fire to watch it blaze up in cool colors, you're stronger than me.

• Dry, dead sticks for kindling. Put the tip of your index finger to the tip of your thumb—your kindling should be thin enough to fit inside that circle, and should be no longer than your forearm.

• Matches or a butane lighter.

5. Is everything dry? If not, you'll have to work a bit harder to make your fire.

• If your wood is mostly dry but you can't find dry kindling (or don't have much kindling at all): Unfold a few sheets of newspaper and, beginning at a corner, roll each sheet tightly on a diagonal. Then tie a loose knot in the long roll of paper. Make three or four of these newspaper loops to start—they'll burn longer than wadded-up paper.

• If your kindling situation is okay but the wood is damp: Ideally the logs should be split, because the wood inside is probably dry enough to catch fire. Handling an ax, however, is probably not within the scope of your talents if you're reading this. If you want to see some fine ax wielding, I refer you to Charles Bronson in *The Magnificent Seven*—but there's no reason for you to take up that kind of challenge as an upstart novice. You can make do without splitting the wood: First, choose the log that seems driest (keep in mind that the smaller logs are more likely to be wet all the way through) and arrange its moist brothers near the fireplace, end to end, single file. Follow the directions in step 6 below, but remember that your slightly damp wood must be a) surrounded by constantly replenished kindling until it actually catches fire and can burn on its own, and b) alone in the fireplace for a while (give the other pieces of wood some time in front of the fire to dry).

6. Once you've answered the questions above to your satisfaction, you're ready to start setting fire to things.

The Easiest Way to Lay a Fire

1. Set two medium-sized logs in the grate, parallel to the back of the fireplace and not too close to it. Make sure the logs have at least two inches of breathing room between them.

2. Make six to eight newspaper loops and stuff them between and under the logs, leaving some space between the loops, and enough paper sticking out for you to light.

3. Lay a handful of kindling in a single layer on top of the two logs and the newspaper.

4. Lay another log on top of all this at a jaunty angle.

5. Light the paper sticking out between the two bottom logs—at both ends and in the center.

At this point, you should be enjoying a pleasant fire in no time, unless the wood is wet. If the wood is wet: Again, lay your first log in the fireplace alone (or else you'll produce a room full of smoke), and replenish the supply of kindling and newspaper until the log dries out enough to catch fire. Once it does, let it burn merrily for at least five minutes before you lay more wood on.

Troubleshooting

There's a lot of smoke. Either your damper is still partly shut or your chimney is cold. Cold chimneys have a hard time sucking up smoke at first. If your chimney is on the outside of the house, one way to warm it up (before you light your fire) is to light a piece of cardboard and hold it up inside the chimney until it becomes foolhardy to hold it any longer.

The logs aren't really catching and there's a lot of smoke. You probably have some wet wood or some green wood (logs that haven't been laying around dead long enough for all the water inside them to dry up). Don't feel too stupid— green wood isn't actually green. It's fresh-looking: tan in color like lumber (what you don't want) as opposed to gray, like firewood (what you do want). If you thunk two pieces of green wood together, you will hear a noise like *thud*. The noise you want to hear, the noise good logs make, is more like *clink*. In the future, look for what is called "seasoned" wood. Seasoned wood is usually dark gray or has dark gray spots, with clearly visible age rings.

If you've laid a fire with a lot of green or damp wood, pretty much the best you can do is use lots of kindling and paper at the base of the fire, blow mightily on it to create a draft (and chase the smoke up the chimney as opposed to into the room), and put the rest of the wood close to the fire to get hot and dry.

I'm tired and want to go to bed. When it's time to extinguish the fire, scatter the logs and distribute ash over everything to smother the embers. Leave the damper open until you're sure every last little bit of the fire is out, though, or you'll wake up to fire alarms and a huge cloud of smoke.

How to Make a Good Fire at a Campsite

Everybody wants a federal tax refund and a one-match campfire. As it happens, there is a formula for an almost foolproof one-match campfire, which seems to have been developed during the enlightened years that followed my generation's campfire dark ages.

The conventional wisdom used to be that the tepee (or the pyramidal stack of Civil War rifles if you were at gifted kids' camp) was the no-fail formation: kindling below, long logs leaning over it with the bottom end in the dirt and the top end touching all the other logs in tepee-esque formation. (Actual tepees, of course, are much more complicated than this, but the tepee campfire was neither the first nor the last time the Native American heritage was dumbed-down for the perverted purposes of summer camp.) The newfangled school of thought, however, proudly—some might say arrogantly—declared victory over the tepee some years ago with the log cabin formation.

Just to be ornery, here's how to do both. Next time you go camping you can kick it old-school tepee-style.

General Rules for All Campfire Builders

A campfire is composed of four kinds of materials, all of which should be gathered before you light a match.

• Tinder: Light bits of things that will catch fire quickly—dead pine tree needles, grass, paper, leaves. Along with kindling, your tinder is the most important part of a quick, quality fire: Gather at least two big handfuls. If you have a good knife, try scraping bits of bark off some of your kindling—many people say bark scraps are the best tinder ever. I prefer dead pine needles, but then, I also prefer the tepee.

• Kindling: Good kindling in the great outdoors is smaller than the kindling you'd use in a fireplace. While you almost wouldn't bother throwing little dead sticks from shrubs and bushes into a fireplace fire, for a campfire those little bitty pieces of dead wood are your bread and butter. Kindling means small sticks of varying lengths and sizes, but nothing thicker than your thumb. Again, find as much of this stuff as you can.

• Sticks: You want to try to find at least ten sticks that are halfway between log and kindling in size—if you put the tip of your index finger to the knuckle of your thumb, that's about the right thickness. Make these six to eight inches long, or no longer than your forearm.

● Logs: Your best campfire logs are two to four inches in diameter and up to a foot and a half long, or about the size of a buff woman's arm.

Never, never, never, never, never take wood or wood shavings from a living tree or shrub. Ever. You will make the tree sick, or kill it. Remember the words of the scary apple trees in *The Wizard of Oz* and how deeply they impressed you as a kid: How would you like it if somebody picked things off of you?

If that logic doesn't deter you, the other major drawback of branches ripped off of living trees is that they don't catch fire as easily as branches that have been dead for a while. The same logic that applies to seasoned versus green firewood applies in the great outdoors: Anything you rip off a tree definitely counts as "green" and will have a lot of water in it, so don't use it unless you want to be huddling over a smoky pile of unlit branches in your firepit come nightfall.

Make sure you build your campfire in a safe place—not in the middle of a grassy field in August, for example. A safe place means a spot with no other flammable stuff under or around it. If you're at a campsite, that means the firepit. If you're making your own campsite, you have to take measures to contain the fire. Choose a spot away from overhanging trees and clear it of all grass and leaves. Get down to bare earth or rock if you can, and make a circle about a yard wide. This is time-consuming, dirty, annoying work, but it's also just what you have to expect for not using a campsite with a ready firepit. Once you're done clearing your firepit, make a circle of rocks in the center—not around the perimeter. This inner circle is where you will be setting fire to things, and the outer circle of bare earth will prevent the fire from spreading.

Some people like to use a hubcap or metal trash can lid upon which to build their campfire in the wild, but you have to wonder why anybody would want to haul a hubcap around through the woods. (If you're one of these people, godspeed.) Admittedly, there's one real benefit to hauling around a hubcap: You can make a campfire anywhere you like without having to clear a new firepit down to bare earth every time you make camp, which is a big time-saver.

First Campfire Steps

The major difference between the tepee and the log cabin is how you arrange the bigger stuff, the sticks and logs. These first campfire steps apply to both formations:

1. Form two handfuls of tinder into a softball-sized clump.

2. Put this clump on the ground in the middle of your firepit.

3. Use your kindling to build a small tepee around the tinder. Leave some gaps between the kindling—later you'll be dropping a match through onto the tinder.

The Log Cabin

1. Organize your sticks roughly according to their length, longest to shortest.

2. Find your two longest sticks. Place them parallel to each other on the ground to either side of the tepee.

3. Form a square around the tepee with your two second-longest sticks—the log cabin base coat—by adding them

parallel to each other, with their ends resting on the ends of the first two sticks.

4. Start another layer of log cabin with your next-longest two sticks: lay them parallel to each other, on top of the corners formed by the bottom square of sticks.

5. Keep building up your log cabin walls in ever-smaller squares until the kindling tepee is surrounded. You'll notice there will be gaps between the sticks—these gaps will facilitate the circulation of air to feed your fire.

6. Carefully lay a few sticks over the top to make a loose roof for your log cabin.

7. Put two of your logs on the ground to either side of your log cabin, right snug up against the wall, or as close as you can get without knocking the cabin over.

8. Now kneel next to the whole structure, light a match and shield it from the wind. Take careful aim, and drop the match through the roof of the log cabin, through the gaps in the kindling tepee, onto the tinder below. If you aim well enough you'll have a one-match campfire. If the overlapping wood creates a sort of seven-ten-split problem and you can't drop the match into the structure so it'll hit the tinder, you can carefully flick the match through the gaps in one of the log cabin walls.

9. When the big logs outside the cabin are burning, lay your remaining logs over them.

The Tepee

1. Complete the First Campfire Steps above.

2. Lay three logs in a loose triangle on the ground around the small tepee of kindling and tinder.

3. Make an *uber*-tepee. Use six to eight sticks to create a slightly taller tepee formation over the first tepee—an *uber*-tepee, if you will. The triangle of logs on the ground will help support the *uber*-tepee sticks and keep them from falling over, which as you may remember from camp is the most annoying thing about building a tepee campfire.

4. Light the tinder inside the smaller tepee.

5. Add sticks and kindling to the *uber*-tepee as you see fit. Remember that if you go crazy with this step, you'll have a veritable bonfire before long, so exercise some restraint.

6. Be a destructive pagan fire god. Once the triangle of logs starts to burn you can "crash" your tepee by putting logs on top of the triangle. Of course, while this is arguably the most exciting part of a tepee campfire, you should also remember to do this carefully.

Troubleshooting

Tinder is hard to come by, and I have more big pieces of wood than small pieces. Bad news: The log cabin and the tepee are not the campfire formations for you. You won't be able to build them without lots of smaller sticks and tinder. Instead, you'll have to make a crisscross campfire.

1. Lay down your two biggest logs parallel to each other, about six inches apart.

2. Put all your tinder and kindling in between the two logs.

3. Lay your next-smallest three or four pieces of wood over all this, perpendicular to the first two logs.

4. Put a layer of your next-smallest sticks over that layer, again perpendicularly.

5. Top it off with a last crisscrossed layer of your smallest pieces of wood.

6. Light the tinder and kindling between the two logs at the bottom. The disadvantages of a crisscross fire are: a) you can't build it quite as high as a tepee or log cabin, and b) adding big pieces of wood on top may make the structure collapse, so it's harder to keep it going.

It's raining. You can still build a good campfire in the rain, but you have to take steps to keep your tinder and matches dry. Don't worry as much about keeping the big logs and sticks dry, but do everything you can to protect the smaller stuff. That means stuffing tinder in your pockets or down your shirt or into a plastic baggie. Empty aspirin bottles are good watertight places to store matches on a camping trip; the Boy Scouts of America also recommends painting the tips of your matches with clear nail polish before you leave, although they do not say where eleven-year-old boys should get a bottle of clear nail polish.

Painful as it is to admit, the log cabin is the superior campfire formation on rainy nights. Its walls protect the small stuff (tinder and kindling) inside long enough to dry out the bigger stuff (larger sticks and logs) so that it too can catch.

I'm at risk of freezing to death and this campfire is my only hope of survival. You want a hot fire that will last. So you have a tough choice to make: The log cabin campfire lasts longer, but the tepee tends to burn hotter—most bonfires are born of tepees. If you have lots of wood, you can make an extremely hot, albeit quick-burning fire by digging a shallow hole (no more than six inches deep) in which to lay your firewood. Figure out which way the wind is blowing, then dig a short tunnel into the hole at the most windward corner—the wind will blow into the tunnel and up into the base of your fire.

I want to put out the fire. Do not mess around when extinguishing a campfire—douse every last little flame with water, pee, Budweiser, whatever you have at hand. Then scatter the logs and spread the ashes with a stick, pouring more liquid on them as you do so. If you don't have much water, throw lots of dry dirt—we're talking shovelfuls—on the embers. Don't use moist-looking dirt with dry leaves in it, because ashes can smolder for weeks and those dry leaves are flammable. When you're finished, you should be able to put your hand on the ground around your firepit and feel no heat.

32

How to Make a Good Fire in a Barbecue

The first step for anybody brave or foolhardy enough to assume the responsibility of getting a barbecue going is this: Let go of your pride completely, and assume a sheepish but determined "little old me with all these matches" expression. (Practice this expression in advance if you're going to be grillmaster at a party with anybody's uncle in attendance.) Whether you are a man, a woman, or George Foreman himself, somebody watching you—most likely multiple somebodies—is going to think they can do it better, and they might even suggest as much to your face. Your best recourse is to act as if you'll be gratefully surprised if it all goes well, and then shame your detractors with the stunning decisiveness of your victory.

There are three basic ways to get a barbecue going (from easiest to most challenging): self-starting charcoal briquets, a charcoal chimney, and a lot of lighter fluid.

First Steps for All Grillmasters

Regardless of what method you use, here's what any smart grillmaster has on hand before he or she strikes a match:

• A pair of long-handled tongs for bullying charcoal briquets both cold and hot

• All the other barbecue tools you think you'll need: basting brush, long-handled fork, cooking tongs, spatulas, spray bottle of water (to douse the frisky flames that, inspired by dripping grease, sometimes leap up out of the coals to char your burgers)

• The right amount of charcoal. Unless you've got an enormous grill or you have to cook for about thirty people, you don't normally need a whole ten-pound bag of coals. Here's a good way to eyeball the right amount:

1. Start with as many coals as it would take to cover the lower grill rack completely in a layer one coal deep.

2. If you're working with a hibachi or some other kind of charcoal grill where the bottom rack is the same size as the upper rack, add enough coals to cover one third of the lower rack.

3. If you're working with one of those round, metal, flaming-globe-of-meat grills (most of us are), add enough coals to cover half the lower grill rack.

• Everything you want to grill—marinated, kebobbed, and ready to go on the fire. You don't want to be running back and forth between the kitchen and the yard frantically preparing hamburger patties while the barbecue is flaming up—it's unsafe, plus it robs you of some really prime grillmaster gloating time. You want to be able to start your coals up and chat amiably with your admirers about the quality of the fire, your philosophy of grilling, and how you laid such a good-lookin' set of coals. You want to be able to sip your beer or your lemonade in the cool early evening as the ineluctably fine smell of barbecue begins to waft out of the yard and down the block, filling your neighbors with the sense of quiet satisfaction and nostalgic longing for summertimes past that the smell of a barbecue tends to inspire. You want to be able to relax and enjoy the moments before you set to flipping things and trying to get everything cooked in a reasonable order. You want to be able to savor your grillmasterhood.

Barbecuing with Self-starting Briquets

1. Remove the top grill rack.

2. Pour the proper amount of charcoal into a pyramidal shape in the center of the bottom grill rack. Use your long-handled tongs to assist in the corraling of wayward coals.

3. Light the pyramid from the bottom, using a long match or butane lighter. Light as many coals as you can, all around the base of the pyramid, without burning yourself.

4. Wait for the flames to die down. Take some time to linger near the barbecue, drinking a beer or lemonade, enduring the abuse or admiration of your guests, and gloating about your forthcoming success. During this time be sure to keep pets and kids from going near the fire. You're waiting for the charcoal to develop a coating of gray ash. This can take anywhere from fifteen to forty minutes, depending on how much charcoal you're using.

5. Make an even layer of coals. Once the charcoal is glowing red and gray and you see no flames, use your long-handled tongs to dismantle the pyramid and create an even layer of coals over the bottom rack. You may find that this process makes the coals frisky and causes them to start burning anew, because you're exposing them to more oxygen. If this happens, just wait for the flames to die down again. Biding one's time is the primary task of the seasoned grillmaster, and is much harder to do than flipping burgers.

6. Prepare the top grill rack. Spray, smear, or baste your top grill rack with a thin coating of vegetable or olive oil and put it back in its place over the bottom rack.

7. Do a hand check. Once you've got an even layer of coals glowing red and gray on the bottom rack of your grill, and your top rack is in place, you can perform a temperature check to make sure you're ready to start cooking. Hold your hand right over the top grill rack and count until it becomes uncomfortable.

If you want . . .	You should be able to count to . . .
Burgers that are raw inside and burned black outside	Less than three
Normal edible red meat	Three to four
Chicken	Four to five
Veggies or veggie burgers	Five to six
Everything undercooked	More than six

If the grill is too hot . . .

wait

use your tongs to move the coals farther apart

raise the cooking rack

cover the grill with the vents open for a few minutes, which will diminish the flow of oxygen and encourage the coals to exercise a little restraint

If the grill's too cool . . .

use your tongs to tap some of the ash off the coals or move the coals closer together

lower the cooking rack

add more coals every thirty to forty minutes if you have a lot of grilling to do; add ten coals for every ten extra minutes you think you'll want to cook

Grilling with a Charcoal Chimney

The charcoal chimney is indisputably convenient, but it's gotten a reputation for being the tool of squeamish barbecue novices, those who want to impress everybody by getting the coals going, as long as they don't get too dirty. But there's a growing underground movement of accomplished grillers with charcoal chimneys hidden in the garage, and grill novices are often disappointed to find that setting up a charcoal chimney can be sort of dirty work anyway.

What exactly is a charcoal chimney? It depends on the user. High-end charcoal chimneys are sold in hardware stores and big grocery stores; low-end charcoal chimneys are more improvisational and can be fashioned from a one-gallon coffee can (cut vents around the bottom with a can opener and use a wire coat hanger as a handle) or cut the top and bottom off a half-gallon milk carton (see page 39 for a range of high- and low-end examples).

The good news is that both high-end and low-end charcoal chimneys are infallible and easy to use. The bad news is that between manhandling coals and wadding up newspaper, your hands get dirtier than those of the spotless, grinning barbecue people on the box your new charcoal chimney came in. An aspiring grillmaster must make his or her peace with such ironies. You will find that your best, fastest, most even and excellent charcoal-laying is inevitably done on

Charcoal
above this line

Wadded newspaper
to this line

nights with unexpected rain or when Uncle Bob isn't there to see it. This is your lot now, your destiny. You are a grillmaster. Get used to humility.

Anyhoots, here's how to use your charcoal chimney:

1. Remove your top grilling rack.

2. Set your empty charcoal chimney, be it humble or glamorous, in the center of the bottom rack.

3. Fill the bottom third or quarter of your chimney with wadded-up paper.

4. Pour charcoal briquets in on top of the paper to fill the chimney.

5. Light the paper through the charcoal chimney vents with a long match or butane lighter. If you're using a milk carton filled with coals, just set the carton alight.

6. Wait about thirty minutes.

7. Remove the chimney. When you see the top layer of charcoal glowing red, grasp the handle of the chimney using your long-handled tongs (*not,* obviously, your hands). Pull the chimney up carefully, leaving the glowing coals behind.

8. Spread the coals in an even layer over the bottom grill rack, using your tongs.

9. Prepare the top grill rack. Coat your top rack with cooking oil and put it in place. Let the rack preheat for a few minutes, and you're ready to cook.

10. Do a hand test. If you're cooking different kinds of food, conduct a hand test, as described on page 36–37, to figure out when the coals are the right temperature for your veggie kabobs or whatnot.

Grilling with Lighter Fluid

You badass. Not for you self-starting briquets. Chimneys are for Santa Claus. You want charcoal dust and lighter fluid fumes and a chance to show that goddamned know-it-all Uncle Bob what a real grillmaster looks like. Bring the pain.

1. Spread your charcoal evenly on the bottom rack of the grill.

2. Apply lighter fluid in a long, steady, slowly moving bad-ass stream, making sure to douse every briquet but good. It takes about one second (as in "one Mississippi," not "one sec") to squirt an ounce of fluid, and a good grillmaster calculates the amount of fluid to use in proportion to how much charcoal is in the barbecue: The ratio is two ounces of lighter fluid to one pound of briquets. Of course, you didn't exactly weigh your charcoal before you put it in, but you did buy a bag, yes? How much of the ten-pound bag did you use, maybe a third? Okay. That's about three pounds, so squirt lighter fluid for about six seconds. It's that easy. Experienced grillmasters do this mental math without even realizing they're doing it; they think in base two. Novice grillmasters will think, "Gosh, that's a lot of lighter fluid, isn't it?" It isn't.

3. Light as many briquets as you can without burning yourself, using a long match or butane lighter.

4. Foster the flames. If you added the right amount of lighter fluid and the evening isn't too humid or windy, you shouldn't have to do much else. But if the briquets are slow to start, you can foster the flames by blowing steadily and softly at the bottom of the coals. Do *not* squirt more lighter fluid on after you've already put a match to the charcoals, even if it looks like the coals are out completely. See the Robert De Niro version of *Cape Fear* if you are in any doubt about the potency of a stream of lighter fluid making contact with a small flame—if Mr. De Niro can explode, so can you. If you're really having trouble, wad up some newspaper into three to five small, tight balls, shove those in between the coals at various points around the perimeter and in the center, and set the paper alight.

5. Wait. Smugly. When the flames die down and the coals develop a layer of gray ash, then follow steps 5 through 8 for Barbecuing with Self-starting Briquets, above. You may be a badass but you're not exactly reinventing the wheel.

Troubleshooting

What if I'm done grilling and the coals are still going and I want to go inside? Put the cover over the grill with the vents closed. This will smother the fire. In general, though, you don't ever want to leave anything hot, burning, or smoldering unattended in your yard.

3.

_____

How to Finish a Piece of Furniture

Why You Should Learn This

In your twenties, you begin the lifelong process of collecting furniture. One of the first things you discover about this process is that it's incredibly expensive. Because you're probably not making a whole lot of money yet, the goal is to furnish your place as cheaply as possible without resorting to desperate measures. Mostly you buy things that are held together with screws, disassemble easily, are composed largely of particle board, and fall apart every time you move. At some point you start looking for furniture made of real wood. And that's when you notice something, something puzzling and gratifying: Unfinished furniture is usually quite a bit cheaper than finished.

So you buy the unfinished furniture in an effort to save money, thinking someday you'll paint it, or something. You never do. And one day you look up and realize that you've got a lot of bald wood in your house and you can't get a book off the shelf without getting a splinter. It's finally time for you to learn to finish your furniture.

Finishing furniture is actually a fun project if you're at all crafty or if you tend to get excited (or wander the aisles in a sort of blissed-out fugue state) in hardware stores. It's a bit time-consuming, but not in terms of work hours you'll have to put in—most of the time required is just to allow the finishing materials to dry. If you have a couple of consecutive weekends with spare hours to devote to something like this, it's absolutely worth the effort. There's a peculiar pleasure to be found in pointing out a piece of furniture in your home and declaring with false modesty—or outright pride—"I finished that myself."

How To

Decide What You Want the Furniture to Look Like

There are plenty of ways to finish a piece of furniture, and which way is best will depend on what the piece is, and how you intend to use it.

The first question to ask is, do you want to stain the wood? Stain is a layer of color that seeps into the fibers and dyes them. You want to stain the wood if:

- You want an unusual color, like, say, a reddish or greenish stain

or

- You want to make the wood darker

and

- The piece of furniture in question is made of fairly good-quality wood to begin with.

A stain is easy to apply—you pretty much just brush it on—but certain types of wood are better than others for staining—such as walnut, birch, ash, and maple—whereas other types of wood look better with a natural finish, like oak, teak, and pine. And unfortunately, you can't make inexpensive wood look like expensive wood by staining it. That means don't apply mahogany-colored stain to pine furniture, it looks ridiculous.

The next question to ask is, how do you want to protect the wood? This is where the finish comes in. Basically, there are *built-up finishes* and *penetrating finishes.* Built-up finishes take more time to do, but are also more scratch-resistant—essentially you're putting a layer of shiny, hard film over the wood. Something like a coffee table probably needs a built-up finish. If you want to preserve the feel of the wood itself and the piece is something that won't be in a high-traffic area, a penetrating finish is better. Penetrating finishes are oils that soak into the wood and harden the fibers. A bookcase is a good candidate for a penetrating finish.

Some stains are incompatible with some finishes, and there are many different types of built-up and penetrating finishes, all of which makes your decision a little harder. Built-up finishes include lacquer, polyurethane, varnish, and shellac, each of which has a different look and feel. Some built-up finishes actually need to be sprayed on as opposed to painted on, like most lacquers and enamels. Spray-on finish is not a job for a first-timers, so that whole can of worms won't be opened here—the instructions that follow are only for finishes that can be applied by hand. You should ask the most knowledgeable-looking assistant at your local hardware store which particular stain and finish they recommend. That person should make his or her recommendation based on the following factors:

- What type of wood you have

- Whether or not you want to stain it

- What kind of time you have

- How big the piece of furniture is

- Your personal comfort level with stuff like sandpaper and chemicals

- How much stuff you want to buy (staining and then applying a built-up finish will cost you more in materials and time than just a layer of penetrating finish)

- The value of the furniture itself (for instance, applying three coats of built-up varnish to your $25 unfinished pine bookcase might not be worth the time and effort, as opposed to an easy application of Danish oil, or paint, which will look just as nice)

Gather Your Weapons

In addition to whatever finish and/or stain you choose, you'll also need:

- Newspapers

- Rubber gloves—you don't really want to touch most of this stuff

- Medium (60 to 80 grit), fine (100 to 150 grit), and extra-fine (220 to 280 grit) sandpaper, at least two packages of each. If you have an especially large piece of furniture, buy more sandpaper.

- A sanding block. Sanding blocks are also available at the hardware store: It's a little block that you wrap the sandpaper around to help provide even pressure while sanding. Don't try sanding without it; you might wreck your furniture and it'll take much more time and elbow grease. Some crafty types staple sandpaper around a chalkboard eraser to use as a sanding block, but it's probably easier just to buy one ready-made.

• Some wide, round plastic containers

• Solvent for cleaning your brushes. What kind of solvent you get depends on what kind of materials you're using—again, just ask the hardware store person.

For staining you'll need:

• A damp sponge (probably . . . some stains don't require you to dampen the wood first, so check the instructions on the label)

• One or two two-inch chisel-end paintbrushes—either natural or synthetic bristles are fine, but avoid the cheapie foam brushes

For a penetrating finish you'll need:

• Lots of clean cotton rags (old bedsheets and towels are good)

For a built-up finish you'll need:

• An additional two-inch chisel-end paintbrush

• Tack cloth (this is basically a fine, sticky cheesecloth)

Set Up a Work Area

Find an uncluttered, sheltered spot that has good ventilation and light, and spread two to three even layers of newspaper on the floor. A garage, covered patio, or screened-in porch with lots of light and cross-ventilation is good; your apartment in the middle of winter is pretty bad. The backyard is less than optimal, since inevitably once you've got two layers of really nice finish spread on, a bug will fly into it.

Have your materials right at hand on a shelf or low table—if you leave stuff on the floor, you may step on it or spill it. Keep your sanding materials separate from your staining and finishing materials (that is, keep the brushes out of the room while you're sanding so grit doesn't get into the bristles).

Sand the Furniture

This is actually the most important part of finishing furniture, and it is done in several steps. First start with the medium sandpaper and sand in short, straight, fairly light strokes at a slight angle against the grain, applying even pressure all the way through the stroke. Using long strokes may seem more efficient, like you're covering more ground at once, but it's hard to keep your arm pressure consistent on long strokes; as you reach farther away, you inevitably lighten up a bit with the sandpaper, which gives you uneven results.

Some important sanding tips:

• Stand perpendicular to the grain of the wood of the furniture, so that your sanding strokes go left-right, rather than forward-back. If you sand forward-back you're more likely to apply a lighter pressure at the end of each stroke.

• Rotate the furniture so that the surface you're sanding is always horizontal—stand a table on its side to get the legs, put it upside down on the floor to get the underside, and so forth.

• On a wide surface, work from side to side rather than end to end.

• Sanding strokes should overlap by half the width of your sanding block.

• When you're sanding close to an edge, don't allow the sanding block to go more than one quarter of an inch or so over the edge with each stroke, or you'll inadvertently round off the edge.

Sanding with the coarser paper at an angle will scrub away glue, dirt, and most stains. It'll also leave scratches all over the wood, but don't panic, because the next two steps will smooth it out.

Dust the furniture off with a brush or cloth. Then sand the

piece again, this time going with the grain and using the fine-grit sandpaper. Once again, dust the furniture off with a brush or cloth. Then sand the entire piece a final time going with the grain and using the extra-fine-grit sandpaper. At this point the wood should be looking pretty smooth. If you want to test for rough spots (and you probably do) get a cheap pair of women's hose, pull it over your hand, and run the hose over the furniture. Any remaining rough spots will snag the hose, and you can go back with the extra-fine sandpaper and smooth them down.

When you finish your final sanding step, it's important to clean the furniture and your work area as well as you can. Dust the furniture thoroughly with a clean cloth, paying special attention to the inside corners on bookshelves or any joints. Move the furniture out of the way and remove the top layer of newspaper from the floor, with all the sanding particles wadded up in it. Brush the furniture off thoroughly, leave the room for a few hours (you'll need a rest at this point anyway) so all the particles can settle to the floor, and sweep, or better yet, vacuum. You don't want little sanding bits to drift into your stain and your finish.

Stain the Furniture

If you're not staining the wood, of course, you can skip this step. (There are some penetrating finishes that actually include a stain, which is pretty convenient.) Follow the instructions on the label for the particular kind of stain you're using—how you prepare for the staining coat and actually apply it varies from type to type. There are some staining tips that should be helpful no matter what kind you're using:

• Before using a new brush for the first time, flip the bristles with your fingers vigorously to shake any lint and loose bristles off.

• If you haven't already mentally broken the furniture up into sections, now's the time to do it, since you need an order of attack for staining and for finishing the piece. You may want to start with the less visible parts of the furniture first—the underside of the table or shelf—then do the back, the legs, the sides, and the top or most visible part last.

• For each section, pour a small amount of stain out of the can and into one of your big plastic containers—it's more manageable and portable, and usually has a wider opening into which to dip your brush.

• You don't want to get your brush super wet because that increases the chances of applying stain unevenly, which gives you dark spots in some areas. For most stains you want to get your brush wet to about halfway up the bristles. For fast-drying stains, however, get the brush as wet as possible and do rapid, soaking strokes with the brush (for a fast-drying stain, in fact, you may want to get a wider brush than the two-inch).

- Brush the stain on in sweeping, long, back-and-forth strokes, moving with the grain.

- Don't overlap strokes.

- Work from end to end or side to side, rather than from the center out.

- Always try to make the section you're working on horizontal. There may be times when you can't avoid doing a vertical section; in those cases, work from the bottom up, with continuous strokes.

- The ends of boards (you'll find these at, for example, the edges of many tables and at the corners of most bookshelves) have more exposed fibers: These end grains will soak up more stain and make the edges look darker than the surfaces if you're not careful. Apply stain very lightly to these areas. If you're working with something like a penetrating oil-based stain—a stain that you apply liberally, allow to set, and then wipe off the excess—wipe off the end grains first, and then do the surfaces.

Most stains should be left overnight to dry completely, so at this point you may want to consider your work done for the day and take a breather. In fact, you may want to break up a finishing job by doing the sanding and staining one weekend and the finishing the following weekend.

Apply Penetrating Finish

This is the easiest thing in the world to do. Okay, not the easiest. Brushing your teeth is easier.

• Working section by section again, pour finish from the can or from a plastic container directly onto a section of the furniture. Using a plastic container may be preferable because it's smaller and more portable and a little easier to handle. Also, you can't accidentally tip too much finish out if you've only got so much in the container to begin with.

• Wearing your rubber gloves, use a clean cotton rag to spread the finish liberally over the whole section, working with the grain. Use enough finish that there's a fairly even coating over the whole section.

• Allow the finish to soak in for fifteen to thirty minutes, or whatever it says on the label.

• Wipe up the excess and move on to the next section.

• The section you're working on should be horizontal, if possible, so that the finish can sink in. If you can't make a particular section horizontal without something horrible happening, work from the top down in short strokes.

When you're done with the whole piece of furniture, buff it all over with a clean rag. Spread all the used rags out to dry thoroughly before you throw them away, because the rags may be flammable.

Apply Built-up Finish

A built-up finish takes more time for two reasons: First of all, you have to use two or three coats, each of which takes some time to dry. Second and importantly, you have to sand the whole piece with extra-fine sandpaper between coats (except after the final coat). It may seem counterintuitive to put a coat of finish on just to sand it again. But that's how built-up finishes work: You're applying a couple of layers of something glossy and slick, and for each successive glossy layer to stick to the one underneath it, you need to resand the piece slightly to provide fine scratches for the glossy stuff to sink into. Follow the directions on the label in terms of how much time you'll need to allow for the furniture to dry before sanding.

With built-up finishes, it's important that the whole piece of furniture be absolutely clean and free of dust. Grease from your fingers will spoil the finish, and dust will get trapped underneath the finish for all eternity. Likewise bugs. So use a tack cloth to rub the furniture thoroughly all over before you do anything. Also, if you're using a brand-new brush, make sure to give it a good workout—flip the bristles and rub them against your fingers to shake off dust and loose bristles.

The first coat you apply doesn't need to be the most beautiful and well-spread coat, since it's really sort of a primer. Still, work as evenly and thinly as you can, going in sections over the furniture. Again, it's best to do the whole underside before you work on the more visible parts. Here's what you need to know in terms of technique:

- Pour the finish into a separate plastic container.

- Dip your brush only about one-third of the way into the finish.

- Wipe excess off the brush against the inside of the container (not the rim) to avoid bubbles in the finish.

- Each brush stroke should have two parts: First, hold the brush at a forty-five-degree angle and stroke the finish on in one direction, going with the grain. Use only a light pressure—pressing down too hard will make bubbles. Then tilt the brush back to a ninety-degree angle and stroke back over the area with the tip of the brush.

- Work with the grain from the center to the ends, and avoid overlapping strokes.

When the whole piece is coated, let it dry for the recommended amount of time (check the label)—this could be a couple of hours or overnight, depending on what kind of finish you use. When it's dry, you get to resand the whole piece of furniture, you lucky dog. Grit your teeth and do your duty. Fortunately, the sanding doesn't need to be too intense—you're not sanding all the way down to bare wood. Go with the grain and use just enough pressure to make fine scratches all over the surface. Brush the piece of furniture off well with your tack cloth, and apply the next coat of finish, which should be more even and deliberate and careful than the first one, because each successive coat is more important to the finished look of the furniture.

If at this point you're exhausted and sick of sandpaper and the smell of varnish, you can stop after the second coat. But for a really nice-looking built-up finish it's better to resand and reapply so you have three coats. Three thin coats are better than two thick ones.

When the final step is done, you've accomplished something that improves not just the look of your house, but also your biceps and triceps, and possibly your moral character. Once the piece of furniture is finished, position it proudly (even if it didn't turn out absolutely perfect) and invite people to admire your handiwork. You've made that furniture into a good-looking piece that you'll own for years—in fact, even when it doesn't work with anything else you own and it's falling apart, you'll find it hard to say good-bye and consign it to the dump. It's yours now in a way it wasn't before. So give it a little pat and give yourself a pat too.

Troubleshooting

I just applied a layer of finish and there's a bug/piece of dust/bubble in a really noticeable spot, what do I do? There's a way to fix minor specks like this. It's called "picking," and it can only be done when the finish is still wet. Use a clean sliver of wood to touch the offending particle— a bubble will disappear, anything more solid will cling to the piece of wood. The finish should then flow together on its own around the spot.

I just applied a layer of finish and there's a brush bristle in a really noticeable spot, what do I do? Poke at it with your wet brush—the bristle should stick to it and you can pull it off. Then do a quick swipe with your brush to smooth the spot out.

4.

How to Get a Raise

Why You Should Learn This

If you're unhappy with your salary, your boss probably doesn't know it, simply because she or he isn't constantly on the lookout for signs that you want or deserve more money. From your boss's perspective, when you accepted the job you knew what the salary was, and aside from promotions and the standard yearly satisfactory-performance upgrades, the company has no reason to throw more money at you. It's always in the company's interest to get as much as it can from employees for as little money as possible.

That said, if you can make an intelligent, provable case for getting a raise, you should. It's always in your best interest to be paid what you're worth.

How To

Make Sure You Deserve One

You deserve a raise if:

• The responsibilities and expectations of your job have grown well beyond what they were when you took it. For example, if there were layoffs and you took on duties that were formerly part of somebody else's job description.

• You make less than other people in your field and geographic region. Salary surveys for various fields are available on the web, and if your department subscribes to any trade publications, chances are good that in a recent back issue of one of those magazines you'll find a for-the-trade survey of what people in your field are making—many trade magazines do this sort of survey once a year, or once every two years. Use the web as well as the trade rags at the library to find out what the average salary is for somebody doing what you do, around where you do it. (Editors in New York, for example, make more than editors in Duluth, and if you work in Duluth, you can't demand a New York salary.)

• You made (or saved) the company a lot of money. Are you the top-grossing salesperson by a long shot? Did you pull in a big-money client that yanked your company back from the brink of ruin? Did you revolutionize bookkeeping in your department so that costs are way down? Have your last five risks paid off hugely? If you saved or made the company a lot of money by doing something different or going beyond the call of duty, you are entitled to some form of compensation.

It's harder to make a case for a raise if all you can say is that you did a killer job on your last presentation or project. You want to be able to point to a series of successes. And more importantly:

Make Sure You Can Prove It

Put some time into collecting and presenting your evidence.

• Know how your boss defines success. There are measures of success for every job description—your boss may have defined some for you at your last performance review. Know what your boss thinks are the measures of success for your job, and decide whether you've blown them out of the water. Say you were supposed to increase traffic to your company's website by 10 percent this year. If you met that goal, you are doing your job. But if you increased traffic by 15 percent and did it under budget, you can show your boss how much you exceeded expectations. Anticipate your boss's objections by thinking about it from his or her perspective: Meeting goals is annual performance review material. Exceeding them is raise material. You want to emphasize any instance in which you've exceeded expectations, whether by leaps and bounds or just leaps.

• Do the numbers. If you can calculate how much of a difference you've made—financially or otherwise—do so, and use that as evidence. Nothing convinces like numbers. Do a little research and number-crunching so you have something to point to.

• Be specific. Don't say that sales are up. Go month by month and show how you drove them up.

Regardless of how much information you're able to compile on your performance, for your boss's easy edification, keep it short and to the point. You may want to create a one-sheet summary with bullet points and graphs that explain or show what you've done that deserves more money. One or two sheets of paper with incontrovertible facts on them are easier for your boss to digest (and wave in front of his or her superiors to make your case) than a massive report. One way you could think about organizing such a "one-sheet" is this:

• Section 1: List four of your job responsibilities or expectations (look at your last performance review, or your résumé, if you've been that frustrated lately) in simple, stripped-down language. Then for each of those responsibilities, detail a specific way in which you've done better than was required.

• Section 2: Make a bulleted list of other, more general accomplishments over the past two quarters, providing actual numbers wherever possible. If you know graph- and chart-making software, it never hurts to have visual evidence.

• Section 3: If your salary is lower than the industry average, provide evidence (with citations). A bar graph can be helpful here, if it's not too depressing, showing what one to three sources have cited as the average salary for what you do compared to your current compensation.

• Section 4: Make a bulleted list of any skills you may have picked up that have improved your performance or benefited the company. Skills increase your market value, but more than that, good bosses know how much time and money it takes to train an employee. By making your boss aware of how much training went into making you the superstar that you are, you are implicitly reminding him or her how much you'd cost to replace, and how much the company has invested in you already.

• Section 5: Make a list of goals for yourself, ways in which you're going to kick even more ass over the next two quarters. This shows your boss that you're not just asking for more money because otherwise you'll quit, you're asking for more money because you see yourself developing in a bigger direction. Think about it: A smart boss would rather spend money on a committed and forward-thinking employee than a disgruntled one. The disgruntled one isn't a good investment because he or she's got one foot out the door.

All this may sound overwhelming, but most bosses respond well to evidence of thoughtfulness and preparation. In the end, use your discretion—if you think too many numbers and facts will make your boss's eyes glaze over, decide on the proper amount of information to have on paper and what to have on mental reserve for discussion purposes. Whatever you finally choose to put down on paper for your boss, do not put down how much money you want.

Make Sure the Timing's Right

No matter how shocking a discrepancy you uncover between what you're earning and what you *should be* earning for all your work, don't ever schedule a meeting with your boss in a fit of indignation (about a raise or anything else). Timing is crucial. In addition to your own performance, you need to think about your company's recent performance, because the financial health of the company (and more specifically your department) will in part determine how much of a raise you can ask for. The time to ask for a raise is when everything's going well—unless you are seriously overdue for a raise, don't bother asking for it in the middle of a hiring freeze or when the company's laying people off in your department.

Schedule a Meeting with Your Boss

Tell your boss you'd like "to discuss performance and goals." Unless your boss is a moron he or she will see the writing on the wall and know what you're about to ask. For that reason, don't jump him or her with a "surprise" meeting. On the other hand, try not to let more than a week pass between asking for the meeting and actually having it—you don't want to give your boss too much time to come up with reasons to shoot you down. If necessary, find out if your boss has a clear spot on his or her calendar that week, and ask for that time slot specifically.

Again, timing is all-important. You probably know your boss's weekly mood swings and when they happen—some bosses are good for nothing by Friday, others don't really gear up until Thursday afternoon. Try to schedule your meeting for a time when you know your boss will be prepared (schedule-wise and brainwave-wise) to hear you out.

Know What You're Asking For

Your numbers and your research serve two purposes: One is convincing your boss to give you a raise, and the other is giving you an idea of what you can ask for. When you walk into your boss's office you'll need to be armed with three important numbers:

• The raise you plan to ask for. This should be a little higher than your research and numbers lead you to think you deserve.

• The raise you think you deserve.

• The raise you'd settle for. Keep in mind, of course, that your boss may refuse your request for a raise outright—he or she can do that.

A smart move, once you know those three numbers, is to figure out how those numbers are expressed as percentages of your current salary. That way you can ask for a 7 percent raise, which sounds less startling than a $4,000 raise.

Make Sure You Ask Nicely

Again, your salary simply is not the most important thing on your boss's mind (the most important thing on your boss's mind is probably his or her *own* salary), so you should approach this as an opportunity to educate your boss, not challenge or shame or beg.

Practice what you're going to say in advance. In the shower the week before your meeting, pretend you're dressed and sitting in your boss's office, and talk to him or her. Smooth out your opening remarks and practice how you want to phrase the actual compensation issue. The time to start stuttering is not when you're talking about numbers.

You've taken the time to put together the documentation; bring two copies and suggest that the two of you use the one-sheet as an agenda or set of talking points for the meeting. Let your boss know you'd like to go through each point, and try not to let him or her rush you through it. At the end of the presentation, you can say, "As you can see, I've put a lot of thought into what I've contributed to the company, and I'm proud of what I've accomplished here. I'd like to discuss how these accomplishments can be reflected in my compensation."

Know What to Do After You Ask

What you do, of course, depends on what your boss says.

• If your boss says he or she needs some time to think about it: Thank them for thinking about it and suggest meeting to discuss the issue again in a month. That way neither of you are on the spot. Don't be disappointed that you didn't get an immediate answer: Keep in mind that most managers have to run things like this past HR, their own boss, and/or the bean-counting department before they can give a definite yes. That said, it's your responsibility to follow up and make sure you have that second meeting.

• If your boss says yes: Make sure you put out and actually do the best work you can, or you can kiss the next two standard annual performance review raises good-bye.

• If your boss says no: Don't give up yet, and don't quit your job yet.

  • Find out why. You shouldn't have to give your boss the third degree, but after all that preparation you deserve a straight answer. What you really want to know is whether it's a performance issue or a budget issue—either way, it's something you can work with. Ask your boss what you can do to improve your chances of getting a raise at some point in the next year. See what he or she says. If you hear a lot of waffling on the issue and you know it's not your performance, you may want to discuss alternatives to money: more vacation time, a better title, an assistant or a share of the department assistant's time.

  • Be patient and persistent. You've planted the seed in your boss's mind and that's half the battle. There may have been timing, staffing, or budget issues beyond your control, or your boss may be one of those types who has to chew on new information for a while. Raise the issue again in a different quarter and see what happens. If after nine months you still haven't received compensation of any kind for an outstanding performance, it may be time to look elsewhere.

5.

How to Order Wine at a Restaurant without Getting Stiffed

Why You Should Learn This

All the prices on all the wine lists at all the restaurants in all the world are marked up, sometimes significantly. You probably already knew that or could reason it out on some level, since it makes sense from a business perspective for the restaurant. While it makes perfect sense, however, this common practice can mean not-so-great things for you as a customer.

The least expensive wines are usually marked up the most; for example, the house wine probably costs the house $5 to $7 a bottle, and is sold for anywhere from $10 to $20. For that reason alone, ordering wine at a restaurant can mean getting not-so-great quality at a price for which you could reasonably expect better—and the proposition gets worse as the quality of the wine list itself declines. It's not that the restaurant owner is a bad person. You just want to be able to outfox the system, because it means you'll get a good value on your wine, and by extension your meal.

How To

Order a Bottle

If there are three or more people at the table who will probably want two glasses of wine each, it's a better deal for all of you to agree on a bottle as opposed to ordering by the glass.

Note the verbiage: It's a better *deal,* but it may not mean that each of you gets to drink the absolute perfect complement to what you're ordering for dinner. Much is said about the appropriateness of particular kinds of wines for particular kinds of food, and lots of strict-sounding rules have been established. Alas, far less lip-service has been paid to developing a good set of guidelines for choosing the right bottle of wine for a group of friends at a restaurant who are ordering different things from the menu.

Narrow Down Your Choices

Say you've all decided to get a bottle. Since you're all interested in getting a good deal on the bottle, all you really have to decide as a group is what color, and what general charac-teristics you'd like the wine to have (a heavy red? a fruity white?). The best first step is to open the wine selection up to the table, so everybody can share their thoughts about what they like and what they're planning to eat. Some helpful ideas not necessarily based on any kind of wine orthodoxy:

• If you can get the group to agree on a color, that's half the battle. It's probably fair to go by majority rule on this issue.

• It's useful to think in terms of lighter wines for lighter meals (fish in herb sauce, veggies, grilled chicken) and more robust wines for heavier meals (steak, fish or chicken in red, creamy, or heavy sauce), and work out whether most people are eating light or heavy that night. If only one person is getting the steak and everybody else is getting a salad with vinaigrette, the steak-eater should graciously agree to drink a Chardonnay.

• If that approach leads to some awkward matches, like steak and Chardonnay, then think about picking a wine in terms of offsetting what most people's food *tastes* like rather than how heavy it is.

If most people are eating something:	Try a wine in either color that's:
Leafy or bitter	Fruity or sweet (a Cabernet or Chardonnay)
In tomato sauce	Dry or off-dry (Sauvignon Blanc, Pinot Noir)
Lemony or otherwise acidic	Acidic (Pinot Grigio)
Spicy	Off-dry or slightly sweet (Riesling, Merlot)
Meaty or fatty	Tannic (Shiraz, red Zinfandel)

• If that sounds too complicated, order wine from the same region as the food. If you're at an Italian restaurant, order southern European wine. If you're at a French restaurant, order northern European wine. If you're at a Mexican restaurant, order Spanish wine, or wine from the New World. In an American or "all-purpose" restaurant, try the California, Australia, or New Zealand wines. This should help narrow your choices at least a little bit.

Stay Away from the House Wine

Unless you ask the server for a recommendation and he or she says, "Actually, the house wine here is really unusually excellent," there's a better value to be had on the wine list somewhere.

Order Something in the Median or Low–Median Price Range

This requires some eyeballing of the entire list and a little mental math. Scan the list: What price do you see most? The cheapest third of the wine list has the highest markup; the most expensive third of the wine list probably has the lowest markup, but that doesn't matter because you probably still can't afford it. Choose something in the middle or just a few dollars above it. Here's an example: If most of the wines are in the $30 range and there are a few in the low twenties, a few in the forties, and one or two in the fifties and sixties, the absolute least you should spend on a bottle of wine is $28, and a better bet is probably around $35.

Ask for a Recommendation

Waiters are supposed to know their stuff, and they almost certainly know the menu and the wine list better than you do. Some people are reluctant to ask for a recommendation because they think the waiter will just try to upsell them on a more expensive wine than they want. But it's not like buying a used car—if the waiter suggests something too steep, just say, "I think we're looking for something in a lower range," and if he or she is any good, they'll come up with something you can afford. If he or she doesn't, then act like you decided not to order wine after all—it sounds crass, but they'd rather sell you less expensive wine than not have any wine on the bill, so the waiter will probably try a little harder to make a recommendation in the range you suggested.

Remember the Clichés

If all else fails, some wine drinkers swear by this easily re-membered rule of thumb: Order the Côte du Rhone or the second-cheapest Spanish red.

6.

How to Parallel Park in Three Breathtakingly Beautiful Movements

Why You Should Learn This

New Yorkers are notoriously hard to impress. They don't care about fame—they've got celebrities coming out the wazoo. They won't blink an eye at fantastic wealth—if you've heard one story about a lapdog with its own pool you've heard them all. You can't even amaze them with luck or talent—they've got the Yankees, and half the city hates them anyway. But you can make a New Yorker's jaw drop with a truly outstanding parallel parking job.

How To

Understand and Adjust to Reality

You have to know how long your car really is. And however long you think it is, add two feet. Can you still fit into the spot you're eyeing so hungrily? Is it worth spending ten minutes trying?

Movement #1

This is the crucial step: Pull up into position. Unfortunately, almost everybody disagrees about what the best starting position is exactly.

You want to pull up next to the car in front of the space you want, leaving about 2 or 3 feet between the cars. It's important not to underestimate the distance between the side of your car and the one next to you—you're going to need every inch of that space, so don't pull up too close alongside your neighbor. Align the edge of your front door roughly with their back wheel (unless it's a truck or SUV with a longer-than-average distance between the back wheel and back bumper, in which case you should align your back bumpers). Yes, yes, you've heard different. Some people say line up your side mirrors, others say line up your back wheels. These rules seem to have developed during an earlier era, in a world before cars all started looking almost exactly the same, that is, like a Honda Accord.

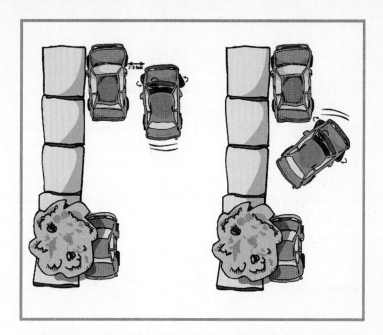

That said, the front-door/back-wheel alignment is one that most of the world's semipro parallel parkers will grudgingly agree works in most situations, even after accounting for personal, "stylistic" adjustments, like wind speed, longitude, and fiberglass versus chrome bumpers.

Before you move at all, turn the wheel twice in the direction of the curb you want to end up next to. You may hesitate after one full rotation, but don't wimp out: Cut all the way. At this point, it's also helpful to unfasten your seat belt so you don't strangle yourself looking backward.

Movement #2, Part One

Shift into reverse and allow the car to glide (not rocket) backward into the spot. Keep going until your front bumper is closer to you than their back bumper. That may sound weird. But think about it. When you start out, with your door next to their bumper, you're actually sitting closer to their bumper than your own. When you start pulling in at an angle, their bumper will get closer still, and then get farther away, until the all-important moment at which yours is nearer. At this point, your car should be about halfway into the spot, lengthwise, and the car behind you will have disappeared from your mirrors.

Movement #2, Part Two

At this time, apply the brakes a bit as you turn your wheel one and a half times in the opposite direction, and continue to glide backward. Come to a stop before you hit the car behind you.

Movement #3 (If Necessary)

Shift out of reverse and tuck yourself into the spot.

This may take some practice, but it's worth it to see the looks on their faces.

Troubleshooting

Which mirror should I be watching? Ah, Grasshopper. A wise man asks not which mirror but which *direction*—backward, in the direction of the car behind you, or forward, in the direction of the possibly-too-close bumpers. Here's a breakdown of where you should be looking, moment by moment:

- During Movement #2, part one (in reverse with your wheel cut toward the curb): If you're parking on the right, look backward until you're about halfway into the spot, then look forward to check whether you're closer to your bumper than theirs. While you're looking backward, remember to put your arm over the passenger seat—professional parallel parkers agree that it looks cool and helps you maintain the turned-around position. If you're parking on the left, you can watch your back end in the driver's side mirror, while keeping an eye out to make sure your front end stays out of trouble. In either case, you will be able to see oncoming traffic—or they'll be able to see you, and if they're not complete idiots they'll understand what you're trying to do and swerve out of your way.

- During Movement #2, part two (in reverse with your wheel cut away from the curb): Look forward until you're sure that your bumper isn't going to scrape up against the car in front of you, then look backward until you're almost touching the car behind you.

- During Movement #3: Look forward.

What if I hit the curb? Alas, that means you won't be able to park in three movements. You have to adjust. Shift out of reverse, wind the wheel one rotation in the opposite direction, and move forward slightly—about a half-foot should do (unless you hit the curb in the forward half of the parking spot, in which case pull out and start over—you were probably pulled up too far when you started backing in). Now wind the wheel back, shift into reverse, and try again. Repeat until you can edge in.

What if I hit (or bump or nudge or otherwise engage with) the car behind or in front of me? If you're asking whether or not you need to leave a confessional note, that is a question you and your conscience must decide alone. Cars are built with bumpers for a reason—because when people park cars on the street, they get bumped. Sometimes getting bumped will cause a tiny, infinitesimal scratch or ding. Sometimes not. Sometimes *infinitesimal* is a relative term. If you're really struggling with whether or not to leave a note with your contact information, maybe you should pay attention to that struggle and ask yourself, "Self, what's it all about? Do I really want to do this?" When you've searched your soul for the answer to that question, and you've decided to be an upstanding citizen and write a note, leave your name and a phone number (preferably not your home phone—what if you hit a crazy person's car?) or email address. Of course, some people leave notes like this:

I'm sorry I scratched your car. I'm only writing this note because people are watching me and I don't want to look like a jerk. Happy driving.

Skills That Save Face

7.

How to Dance a "Slow Dance" without Looking Like an Idiot

Why You Should Learn This

The words *slow dance* tend to strike simultaneous hope and despair into our hearts: These emotions are the psychic residuals of eighth-grade dances in the gym, when even if you were asked to dance by somebody, all you could do was lock arms around each other and shuffle awkwardly back and forth for three and a half minutes, avoiding eye contact. *(My arms around his neck; his arms around my waist, at least six inches separating our . . . bodies. Eew, we have* bodies. *I just thought the word* bodies *about me and Scott Pulaski! Okay, okay, don't panic, "Careless Whisper" is on . . .)* Afterward you'd get approving glances from friends, but during the dance you could never remember why you wanted to do this to begin with.

Fast forward to your twenties and early thirties: weddings every five minutes. Your cousin, your former roommate, your best friend, your significant other's best friend, and your ex are all going to get married the same year, you can bank on it. You will go to as many of these weddings as you can reasonably afford. You will move heaven and earth to have a date to at least some of these weddings, or you will hope for a hot bridesmaid or groomsman to hang out with so you don't end up sitting next to your best friend's cousin all night. At some point, at some wedding, you will have to dance a "slow dance." You will feel dumb and awkward, but avoiding eye contact for three minutes is no longer an option because you're not thirteen anymore. Most of us, if so moved, will happily dance to a fast song according to our own peculiar rhythmic and physical druthers, but as for slow songs, shuffling around the floor making little concentric circles doesn't cut it after a certain age.

At the same time, you can always tell which couple has taken ballroom or swing dancing lessons so as not to look stupid at people's weddings anymore: They're counting under their breaths, or looking like they're concentrating really hard—on something besides each other—or worse yet, showing off (like that mean girl at the school dance in *Grease*: "They call me Cha Cha . . . 'cause I'm the best dancer at St. Bernadette's!"). You don't want to look phony or forced. You want to look like you have somebody in your arms that you're reasonably glad to find there, and the two of you are having a pleasant time moving in rhythm to a song that sways and swings a little bit.

How To

Be Honest: Can You Count?

In rhythm, that is? And more importantly, if you can count one TWO three FOUR, can you make those beats *mean* anything for your body? Ideally you'll be able to admit the truth before you ask someone to dance with you. Dig deep: Somewhere inside, you already know whether you have rhythm or not. Some of us just can't count to four in rhythm. Some can count, but they can't translate that ability into physical movements. Unfortunately, I don't think you can be taught to do it, at least not by reading, so you will have to become a Suave Faker. Don't worry, you'll still look good.

If you can already count and move in rhythm, you will just be plain old suave.

Know When and How to Hold 'Em

Take your partner by the hand and go together to a choice spot on the dance floor. You've seen couples in old-school dancing position in movies or ads, but probably not on an actual dance floor unless you go to lots of dances at the VFW.

Still, the old ways are often the best ways: Guys, put your right hand at the small of her back, and take her right hand in your left, at around shoulder level. Gals, put your left hand on his shoulder and your right hand in his left. The fingers don't interlace: He holds his hand out with the fingers pointing toward the wall, and you slide your hand in so that your palms press together. Pull in as close as you decently can, or are willing. Being close together isn't just cozy; closeness makes it easier for whoever's leading to guide the two of you through the dance. Keep your shoulders back, your heads high, and don't stiffen up—especially in the legs.

Now, for the Suave Fakers, anxiety may kick in at about this point. Fakers: Your mission is to enjoy yourself anyway. It's not a contest, unless you, in fact, foolishly got yourself into a contest. You should smile, look your partner in the eyes, and do what comes naturally . . . according to these instructions.

Decide Who Leads

In this day and age, it's not always necessary for the fella to lead, so you may be tempted to skip the issue altogether. But who leads is still an important consideration for one big reason: Whoever leads gets to move forward instead of backward. Needless to say, going forward is easier. For that reason, if it's sort of an open secret between the two of you that one has rhythm and one doesn't (that is, one of you is suave and the other is a Suave Faker), *let the Suave Faker lead.* This may sound counterintuitive. But think about it: The better dancer will be better equipped to keep up with (and if necessary, compensate for) whatever the not-so-good dancer throws at him or her. Following is in many ways harder than leading. When a good dancer leads a not-as-good dancer through his or her paces on the dance floor, it's a challenge, not a dance. A not-as-good dancer won't be able to endure a whole night like that, no matter how good a sport he or she is. Unless you're in a class, the dance floor isn't a fun place to be taught how to move. So the Suave Faker needs to be going forward, and he or she needs to be setting the pace. It's more enjoyable for both of you that way.

In dance classes, the leader always has his or her hand around the non-leader's waist. That's rarely how it falls out in real life with a real couple. Whether it's a woman or a man leading, women naturally tend to reach for the shoulder and men tend to reach for the waist—maybe it's another residual tic of eighth-grade dances, maybe we've all watched too many movies, who knows. The point is, if that's what feels natural, why do a jokey, formal correction ("Whoops, ha ha, other way!") just to follow the rules? In ballroom dancing, it's important to be led by the waist, but since you're not at a contest (you're not at a contest, right?), you can lead from wherever the hell you need to in order to get the job done.

If you are a Suave Faker and your partner doesn't know it

yet, it's acceptable to ask to lead, regardless of gender. If you're not comfortable asking to lead (for instance, if you're a gal and your partner is an older gentleman—the bride's uncle, say—who, you sense, might be a bit bemused by the request), you may want to do your partner a favor and advise him that you'll need some guidance. A considerate partner will oblige as best he or she can.

Start with the Basics

For the first twenty seconds or so of the song, allow yourself a little time to get used to the whole idea of dancing together. Don't start twirling all over the place just yet. Three good things to try in the first twenty seconds of the song—just to get your sea legs, so to speak—are:

Sway side to side in unison in time to the music. This just means rocking back and forth in place, shifting your weight from one foot to the other with each beat. Most Suave Fakers can do this without even having to fake anything yet. So if you're swaying together and things are going pretty well:

Try a step to the side together. A step is simple. While your weight is on, say, your right foot, step your left foot to the side a bit, then bring the right foot over to meet it and keep swaying. Do this at whatever speed feels comfortable (slow, smooth steps are suaver than quick, jerky ones), and don't try to cover too much ground. This is the leader's opportunity to try leading, and the follower's opportunity to learn how to detect his or her cues. For now, don't stress too much about stepping right on the beat. Nobody's looking at you anyway.

"Leading" means nothing more or less than applying a tiny pressure, or cue, in the direction you want your partner to move. So gals, to lead him in a step to the side, you'd apply a tiny push to his shoulder and hand in the right direction as you step. Fellas, you lead by guiding from her waist and hand as you step. If you're following, you may not step at exactly the same time, but that's okay as long as you end in the same place. Do one step, then sway back and forth in place for a few seconds. Then try stepping back to the other side and see if it's easier to give and take cues. Suave Fakers, you are officially dancing at this point. Congratulations. If you get no further than this, you can still have a perfectly debonair presence on the dance floor for the next few minutes. Just step and sway as gracefully as possible, smile at your partner, and make some conversation ("Beautiful night, isn't it?"). If you're feeling pretty confident:

Try a step on a diagonal together. For leaders:

1. While your weight's on your right foot, give your partner his or her cue by applying a little pressure (that is, a tiny push with your hand against your partner's) toward the left and back.

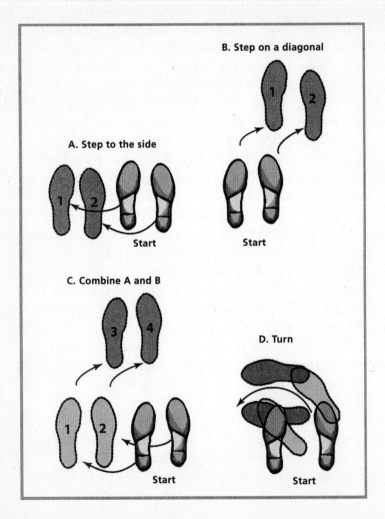

B. Step on a diagonal

A. Step to the side

Start

Start

C. Combine A and B

D. Turn

Start

Start

2. Move forward on a diagonal with the left foot.

3. Bring your right foot to meet your left.

Whoever's not leading will perceive the cue, step back-ward on a diagonal with the right foot and bring his or her left to meet it. Try it and see. Going on a diagonal, as op-posed to straight back, makes it less likely that the leader will step right on the partner's toes before the partner has a chance to realize that he or she has to move backward.

Put the Basics to Music

Once you're comfortable making steps to the side and in a di-agonal, try making sure you're stepping on the beat, or rea-sonably close to it. If you are in any doubt about whether or not you're a Suave Faker, this is the test.

• The beat is probably your standard one TWO three FOUR. Note the emphasis on beats two and four—this is where the rhythmic stress falls in most popular music, from Basie to the Beatles. A beat that goes ONE two THREE four is a march. If you find yourself on the dance floor and the band strikes up a march you're on your own . . . or you're in Germany. The rhythmic stress is your cue to move—in general, when exe-cuting a step, you make your move on the stressed beat. It's easier for everybody that way.

• A step to the side in rhythm (for the leader; followers use the opposite feet) would go like this:

sway R	L foot to the side	R foot to meet	sway L
one	TWO	three	FOUR

• A diagonal step in rhythm (for the leader; followers use the opposite feet) would go like this:

sway R	L foot to forward	R foot to meet	sway L
one	TWO	three	FOUR

Put the Basics Together

Try a step to the side, then a step forward on a diagonal, then sway for a couple of beats.

sway R	L foot to the side	R foot to meet	L foot forward	R foot to meet	sway L
one	TWO	three	FOUR	one	TWO

Rinse. Repeat.

Turn

You can lead your partner in a turn while swaying, by pivoting slightly on the foot that bears your weight, then stepping the opposite foot in the appropriate direction. If you want to do a full circle, go at a slow pace (pivot, then sway in place for a beat or two, then pivot again) so you don't look like you have one foot nailed to the floor.

By now, Suave Fakers should have a basic sense of how little is required of them. It's not necessary to impress your partner with fancy footwork, as long as you move with a slow, sure confidence that assures your partner he or she's in good hands.

8

How to Use a Full Place Setting Properly (Including Chopsticks and Asian Soup Spoons)

Why You Should Learn This

If you want to continue to eat out at restaurants, sooner or later you've got to learn the rules of the table. And there are many. And more people know them and take them seriously than you might think. They may not call you out on it, but you can bet that it doesn't go unnoticed when you make an obvious and possibly gross mistake at dinner. This becomes more and more the case the older you get, and the more clients, colleagues, and business associates you are compelled to wine and dine.

You're probably already aware of the basics, like the "outside-in" rule as it pertains to forks, and the humanitarian prohibition against snapping fingers or whistling for a waiter's attention. Formal etiquette often seems arbitrary and, well, formal, and many formerly ironclad rules have come to be, at best, disregarded and at worst, abused and ridiculed. So it's understandable that you might think it's unnecessary to learn and adhere to old-fashioned dining etiquette. But at a restaurant or a dinner party, there's a fine line between informality and sloppiness. And sloppiness is just flat-out unacceptable as regards food and its consumption. Somebody went to the trouble of laying out a graceful place setting for you and you should live up to the courtesy.

The problem is, sloppiness at the table is also kind of tempting, because being a graceful diner means much more than just knowing which fork to use—in fact, that's the easy part.

How To

Know Your Way Around a Standard Place Setting

Study the diagram on the following page. It should look sort of familiar.

Plates and Bowls

a. Charger or service plate—You don't actually eat anything off of this plate. The waiter will either take it away when

you order or when the main course comes, or the soup, salad, and entrée dishes may be placed on top of it.

b. Salad or appetizer plate—This'll either be on top of the charger, or off to the left.

c. Soup bowl and liner plate—Again, these will probably be on top of the charger or off to one side.

d. Bread plate—The smallest plate on the table.

Glasses

e. Water glass—Typically this is the largest glass on the table.

f. Wineglass or glasses—Your wineglass will probably be a bit closer to you than your water glass. If there are two wine-glasses, the rounder one is for red wine and the slimmer one is for white. If you don't order wine, the waiter will take these glasses away.

Utensils (basic)

g. Salad fork—You'll know it's a salad fork because 1) it's farthest on the outside, 2) it's probably shorter than the fork beside it, and 3) it may have one tine that's a little thicker than the others; if you don't have a salad knife, use that side of the fork for cutting big pieces of lettuce or cucumber.

h. Dinner fork—Regardless of how many forks you may find when you sit down, the largest one is always for the main course, and usually it's the one right next to the plate.

i. Dinner knife—Same deal here as for forks; the largest closest-in one is always for the entrée.

j. Soup spoon—The soup spoon is the largest spoon at your setting, usually laid just outside your dinner knife.

Utensils (fancy)

k. Bread knife—This is the smallest knife on the table; you'll probably find it on or near your bread plate.

l. Dessert spoon and/or fork—These are smallish utensils that are usually set horizontally above the service plate, perpendicular to the rest of your place setting.

m. Salad knife—If there are two knives and neither of them are serrated, the one on the outside is probably a salad knife. Salad knives are a little shorter than dinner knives, with a slightly rounded blade.

n. Steak or fish knife—If there are two (or three) knives and one is serrated (usually it's to the right of the dinner knife, and about the same size), then that's your steak or fish knife. If you don't order steak or fish, the waiter will take the knife away.

o. Teaspoon—If there are two spoons to the right of your plate, it's probably breakfast or lunchtime, and the smaller spoon is a teaspoon, for coffee or tea. At dinner, a spoon is usually brought out with the coffee if it's ordered.

Know the Big Three Rules

They are:

1. Use all utensils from the outside in. On occasion you may, however, have a lazy or distracted waiter who makes this otherwise nonconfusing rule impossible to follow: If you don't order a salad or appetizer, and your waiter does not take your salad fork away before bringing your entrée, then skip over the salad fork (and knife, if you have two knives) and use your entrée fork and knife, the utensils closest in to your plate.

2. Once you've used a utensil, it never goes back onto the tabletop. Rest used knives and forks with their handles on the plate edge, and their blades or tines on the center of the plate. Put used spoons on the saucer or liner plate rather than leaving them in the bowl or cup. If you're done eating, lay your knife and fork together on a diagonal across the rim of the plate, so the waiter knows he or she can clear your plate away.

3. Never gesture with a utensil.

The Napkin

Usually the time to put your napkin in your lap is right when you sit down. If, however, you're at a business lunch and the expectation is that you'll talk or drink a while before getting down to the meal, leave your napkin on the service plate. Dinners at a person's home also call for a bit of decorous hesitation: It's considered polite to wait until the host or hostess has seated him- or herself before putting your napkin in your lap.

Don't tuck the napkin in anywhere, and don't use it for anything more strenuous than blotting your lips. If at some point you get up, leave your napkin on your chair, not on the table.

The Bread and Butter

Don't attack the bread basket until after the busperson brings your water. In fact, it's best not to dig into the bread and butter until after the waiter has made his or her first appearance and taken your drink order, but if there's an unusually long wait you can start.

Deal with the butter first:

• Use your bread knife to put your own smallish portion of butter on your bread plate.

• If the butter is served in a wrapped pat, unwrap your butter and put it on your plate. Then fold the wrapper up and put it near the bread plate's rim.

• Never butter bread directly from the communal butter plate or bowl.

• Put your used bread knife on the bread plate, not the table.

Now the bread:

• Bread is one of the few things at a table that it's acceptable to pick up with your fingers, so carefully pluck your roll or bread slice or what have you from the bread basket. If it's a loaf of crusty bread, you can still break it off with your fingers, but don't pick up the whole loaf and tear off your chunk. Leave the loaf in the basket and try to touch the other slices as little as possible as you pull your piece away.

• Break off a bite-sized piece of bread with your fingers—not your teeth.

• Butter the bite-sized bread from the butter on your bread plate.

• Never butter more than a bite-sized chunk at once, and never bite off a chunk directly from the roll or slice.

The Appetizer or Salad Course

There are two, and only two, courses that are acceptable to cut with your fork: one is salad, and the other is dessert. If you have a salad or appetizer knife, of course, use that. If you get an appetizer that's not a salad, use your salad plate and utensils.

Soup

- When you spoon up your soup, spoon away from you—that is, toward the center of the table.

- You should collect only about three-quarters of a spoonful for each bite.

- Don't put the whole spoon in your mouth; rather, sip the soup out quietly from the side of the spoon.

- It's acceptable to tip the soup bowl away from you a bit to collect the last two or three spoonfuls.

- Unless it's a pretty informal place, don't go dipping your bread in the soup—although soup-soaked bread is really really tasty. If you can't resist the temptation, soak up the last few bites of soup with a corner of bread, and try to look dainty.

- When you're finished, don't leave the spoon in the bowl. Put it on the liner plate or saucer, or if there isn't one, lay the spoon on a diagonal across the rim of the bowl.

The Main Course

The most important thing to remember about the main course is the proper way to cut and fork it. Either of the following is fine.

European-style is what you've seen people doing in those Merchant-Ivory films that take place at Italian boarding-houses. If you're ambidextrous, European-style may be a good choice:

- Hold the fork in your nondominant hand and the knife in your dominant hand.

- Cut off a bite-sized amount with the knife, using the fork (tines down) to hold the food in place.

- Raise the fork to your mouth tines down, leaving the knife in your other hand, blade resting on the plate.

American-style is the way to go if you're not too steady with your nondominant hand, or you don't want to look like an extra in a Merchant-Ivory film:

- Hold the fork in your nondominant hand and the knife in your dominant hand.

- Cut off a bite-sized amount with the knife, using the fork (tines down) to hold the food in place.

- Lay the knife down, with the handle on the rim of the plate and the blade on the plate itself.

- Switch the fork to your dominant hand and raise the food to your mouth, tines up.

American-style may sound tedious, but you'll get used to it. Although you may be tempted to for the sake of efficiency, don't cut all of your food into bites at once. Cut only one or two bites at a time. And don't cut food with your fork.

Dessert and Coffee

If you didn't have adorable little dessert utensils perched perpendicularly over your plate when you sat down, they will be brought out with the dessert itself. Keep your napkin in your lap until dessert is finished, and then put it on the table to the left of the plate. Sometimes the postprandial coffee drinking goes on long after dessert is over; in that case it's acceptable to take the napkin off your lap and put it on the table to be cleared away with the dessert dishes.

Chopsticks

If you still haven't learned to use chopsticks, it's not too late, but this is *definitely* a skill to acquire before you're thirty, if you pick up nothing else useful from these pages. People who use forks at Chinese restaurants aren't exactly breaking the law, but it's still pretty lame. The next time you get Chinese takeout, use the chopsticks to practice these moves at home:

- With your dominant hand, pick up one chopstick as if you were going to write with it, just as you were taught to

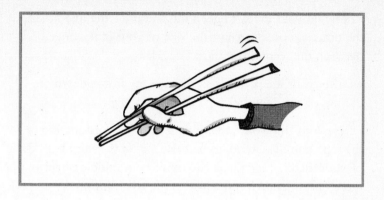

hold a pencil in second-grade handwriting lessons: The side of the chopstick rests on the third knuckle of your ring finger, with the tip of your middle finger holding it in place, and the tip of your index finger on top of the chopstick, just behind your middle finger. The middle of the chopstick should be pressed against the side of your index finger between the first and second knuckle. The pad of your thumb should be holding the chopstick against the side of your index finger, and the tip of your index finger should be right over the tip of your thumb. All this should feel pretty natural, unless you developed bad pencil habits when you were eight. You now have your bottom chopstick in position, and the good news is the bottom chopstick doesn't move.

• Now lift your index finger a bit, and place the middle of the other chopstick against the side of your index finger, between the second and third knuckle.

• Lower your index finger so that the tip presses down on the top of the chopstick.

• Keep lowering your index finger until the forward end of the top chopstick comes to be balanced on the third knuckle of your middle finger, and the tip of your middle finger is more or less sandwiched between the two chopsticks.

• Roll your thumb up over the bottom chopstick a bit, so that you can pinch the top chopstick against your index finger with the tip of your thumb. The pad of your thumb should press against the bottom chopstick, and the tip of your thumb should press against the top chopstick.

• Now try lifting just the tip of your index finger, while continuing to press in with your thumb. When you lift the tip of your index finger, the tip of the top chopstick should move up off the third knuckle of your middle finger. When you press down, the chopstick goes down.

That's all there is to it. You should be able to pick up chunks of food by lifting your index finger, positioning the chopsticks around the food, then lowering your index finger so the chopsticks pinch the food.

Now that you've mastered chopstick usage, there are some basic rules of chopstick etiquette:

• If you had to break your wooden chopsticks apart, it's a good practice to rub the ends against each other a few times to smooth down any splinters. Hold one chopstick straight out, and draw the end of the second chopstick down against the first. Then switch sides.

• Once the chopsticks have taken their inaugural visit to your mouth, they should not be used on any communal plate. If you want another helping of dumplings, use a serving spoon.

• Just like Western utensils, chopsticks should never be placed back on the table after they've been used. Rest them on your plate instead, or if there's a chopstick rest, put the used tips of the chopsticks on it, with the clean ends on the table.

• It's okay to lift your rice bowl closer to your face to facilitate the scooping of rice into your mouth. It's pretty well understood that once the meal's sauces have soaked in, the rice doesn't clump together anymore and it gets hard to eat. It is not okay, however, to lift a plate to your mouth for this reason. You may want to transfer food onto the rice in your rice bowl, and then lift the bowl closer to your mouth.

Hold the bowl by the bottom and lift it to about chin level, a few inches in front of your face.

• Pick up only bite-sized amounts of food with your chopsticks, unless the food comes in big pieces. Dumplings and most sushi, for example, aren't exactly bite-sized, but can still be eaten with chopsticks. Pick up non–bite-sized foods close to one end, rather than by the middle. Lean slightly over your plate and take a modest bite all the way through, being careful not to spill anything (or to spill as little as possible). Rest the other part of the food and your chopsticks against your plate while you chew. Then lift the chopsticks to your mouth and finish the other part.

• Soup dumplings are a little trickier and are usually served with wide porcelain soup spoons. Place the dumpling in the spoon with your chopsticks, then raise both the spoon and the chopsticks to your mouth. Pinch the top of the dumpling with the chopsticks and bite it off. Sip the soup in the dumpling from the end of the spoon. Use your chopsticks to pick the other pieces of the dumpling out of the spoon.

• For big bowls of noodle soup, you can use your chopsticks and your soup spoon in tandem as long as you do it in a controlled fashion. Gather a reasonable amount of noodles between your chopsticks, and drape the noodles just below the chopsticks over the soup spoon, keeping the noodle ends in the broth. Lean over the bowl and bite off the noodles on the ends of your chopsticks, so that the noodles below that bite fall onto your soup spoon. Lower the rest of the noodles back into the bowl—try not to drop them in or you'll splash broth on yourself.

• Don't try to cut anything in half with your chopsticks.

• Don't put the whole bowl of an Asian soup spoon into your mouth. Fill the spoon halfway and sip broth out from the tip.

• Chopstick usage varies at Japanese restaurants. Some people prefer to eat sushi as finger food, using chopsticks solely to remove sushi pieces from the communal plate and to pick off tasty chunks of wasabi and pickled ginger. Look to see what your most-put-together neighbors are doing, and copy them.

Troubleshooting

I dropped something. What now? Pick it up off the floor, if possible, and put it on the edge of the table. Signal the waiter and let him or her know you need a new napkin, fork, or what have you, and he or she will discreetly take the humbled instrument away and bring you a new one. If you can't reach the thing you dropped without getting up or inconveniencing someone, let it lie and just tell the waiter you dropped it.

9.

How to Clean Your Place in Under 45 Minutes, If Friends, Relatives, or Prospective Lovers Are Coming by Unexpectedly, and Soon

Why You Should Learn This

You're hanging out at home in happy sloth, watching "Golden Girls" and wearing dirty socks, when you get a phone call. It's That Person, or Mom, or a brokenhearted friend in need of succor and solace, or a roving gang of your favorite people, and they're wondering if you're up to anything and would you mind if they came over and would you mind if it was soon. Sure, you could insist on meeting them for coffee someplace, but you don't want to seem unwelcoming and unapproachable, so you say yes. And then you look around and your heart does *not* leap up when you behold your humble little sty.

You don't always get to choose when people come over. It's probably best, in fact, that you can't always choose—there's something admirable about a person who can handle a spontaneous home invasion with aplomb. And it's to your benefit to be able to ask friends over for a cup of coffee or a cocktail without having to plan in advance just to get your dishes washed. Impromptu gestures of hospitality are what makes a Holly Golightly out of a Lula Mae Barnes. Spontaneity aside, the best reason to learn how to tidy up your home quickly is to keep other people from finding out you're a slob.

Most of us are slobs. But it's okay. Everybody knows cleaning isn't that fun. I happen to find washing dishes kind of soothing and pleasant—the warm water, the nice-smelling suds—but that doesn't mean I wouldn't rather be snorkeling, or in Italy someplace. We all have better things to do than clean. Usually.

That said, your friends and guests *also* have better things to do than sit around in your mess. So keep your mess to yourself.

How To

It's quite simple. Go as far down this list as you can until the doorbell rings.

1. Gather Your Weapons

• Have a stopwatch, microwave timer, egg timer, or alarm clock at the ready—anything with an actual buzzer

• A bottle of spray cleaner (glass cleaner is best)

• An empty garbage bag

• A roll of paper towels

• A damp sponge or cloth

• A regular dishtowel

• A broom and dustpan

• A large bag—this can be a shopping bag or a garbage bag or a suitcase, whatever you can find first

2. Prioritize

Take thirty seconds (no more, no less) to look around you and decide which looks worse: your place, or you. If you look worse, hie yourself into the bathroom, set your timer for **five minutes** and freshen up. It's better to greet someone at the gates of Gehenna looking good than to rush to the door of an immaculate house looking—and more importantly, acting—as if you've just spent the last twenty minutes polishing doorknobs. People are less likely to remember the mess in your sink than your own frazzled and unwelcoming state.

3. While You're in the Bathroom . . .

There are exactly two rooms a guest is likely to see when they visit: 1) whatever room you show them into to have a seat, and 2) this one. You can close the doors to any other rooms you don't want people to see, but sooner or later somebody's going to need to use your bathroom. The bathroom is always, always the best place to start, and it's where you should spend the first fifteen minutes of any last-ditch cleanup effort.

- Start by setting your timer for **fifteen minutes**.

- *The Towel Trick:* Despoil your bathroom of *all towels* except rack towels, and make those clean ones. Take any and all dirty towels to the hamper. For as long as you have guests, don't have towels hanging from the back of the door, from wall pegs, or over the shower curtain rod. Nothing spoils the illusion of an otherwise decent wipe-down job faster than limply dangling used towels and the mildewy smell pertaining thereto. If your used towels aren't dirty enough for the hamper, fold them and put them temporarily back in the cabinet—you can hang them back up when everybody leaves.

The towel trick is indispensable. Think of it this way: Imagine your friend, in your bathroom, looking for something to wipe his or her hands on. Then imagine the parts of your body that all your dirty towels have touched. Then imagine your friend imagining that.

The other great thing about the towel trick is that it leaves the room with a satisfying tabula-rasa feeling—nothing dangling, nothing damp, nothing but the essentials here.

● *The Ammonia Trick:* Get paper towels and a spray bottle of glass cleaner and wipe down every visible surface—yes, wipe the sink with paper towels, you don't have time for a sponge. For really quick cleanup jobs, glass cleaner is infinitely superior to scrubbing powder, spray-on cleaner, or even those newfangled cleaning cloths. Here are five important reasons why: glass cleaner is quick, it dries fast, it can be used on all bathroom surfaces, it makes things shiny, and the ammonia leaves behind a medicinal odor that enhances the illusion of cleanliness. No, you're not really killing millions of germs. No, you're not really scrubbing anything. You're a slob in a hurry. You don't have time for niceties.

● *The Chrome Trick:* Be sure to use your glass cleaner on all the chrome fixtures and the mirror. Sparkliness is a key element in the illusion of cleanliness.

● Also be sure to lift up the toilet lid and use your sponge or paper towels to make sure all's quiet on the western front.

• A bare floor is better than a skanky bathroom mat. If any of the following adjectives apply to the bathroom mat, remove it from the room: *matted, smelly, sticky, damp, crusty, crumby, hairy, discolored*.

• Empty the bathroom trash into a garbage bag.

• Hairs on the floor? Sweep. Swiftly. If the floor is wet, do not attempt to sweep. Instead, use a damp sponge to wipe up stray hairs.

• Do not find a clever nook for your toilet paper. Do not scrub the shower. Do not mop. Wipe the sink, the fixtures, the mirror, the chrome, the toilet (seat, lid, cover, and base), and get the hell out of there when the timer goes off. You've only got twenty-five minutes left.

4. Move On

Move on to the room where you're imagining your impending visitors will hang out. For most people, that's the living room. If for you that means the kitchen, you may skip to step 5.

• Set your timer for **ten minutes**.

• *The Scorched-Earth Policy Trick:* First, go around the room and put into your trash bag all things that belong in a trash bag. Then look around. If there is anything (bills, letters, newspapers, magazines, odd bits, clothing) sitting on top of anything (floor, desk, table, bed, chair, sofa, TV set) that does not fall into the functional or decorative categories (lamps are functional, framed pictures are decorative, books are both functional and decorative), pick it up and put it into the other big empty bag you found. Once every surface in the room is cleared, put the bag into a closet. If you can't fit it in the closet, put it in the oven. If you're having people over for dinner, put it under the bed. Just find a hiding place for your big bad bag. You can deal with its contents later, after everyone leaves.

• Make sure you have your damp sponge or cloth and your dry dishtowel. Now set your timer for **five minutes** and wipe the following things, either with the dry cloth (for metal, unfinished or finished wood, cloth, or God help us, wicker) or with damp followed by dry (for painted wood, plastic, glass):

1. the television screen and top;

2. all table and desktop surfaces;

3. the stereo top and buttons (better to put guests off by your taste in music than by two inches of dust on the CD player);

4. your bookshelves (this is best accomplished by using the dry dishtowel as a sort of ersatz featherduster—swat at

your shelves and books lightly with one end of the towel).

• Give the couch pillows a good punitive pat down and make the coffee table and end tables neat.

5. Assess Your Situation

. . . And set your timer for whichever applies to you:

• If you followed steps 1 through 4, you have ten minutes left.

• Unless you foolishly violated your time limit in one room or other. If you did, and you find yourself with less than ten minutes, you have a choice to make: You can either resolve to keep your guests out of the kitchen entirely and set to work making everybody a drink, or you can spend the next five minutes doing as much of step 6 as you can. If I were your guest, though, I'd want a drink.

• If you look good enough to have skipped step 2, you have fifteen minutes left.

• If you skipped step 4 because your place is small and everybody's going to be in the kitchen, you have twenty-five minutes left.

6. Make the Kitchen Guest-Friendly

It's not easy, but you may find it helpful to think in terms of what will be within your guests' sight lines:

• They'll probably spend most of their time seated at the kitchen table or standing near a counter. Clear and wipe these surfaces first.

• They will almost certainly look at the floor at some point, whether abashed by your hosting prowess or to avert their gaze when your personal attractiveness simply becomes too overwhelming. Sweep.

• Put your clean dishes away.

• Wash your dirty dishes.

• Make the sink sparkly. Use glass cleaner to make the fixtures shine—the Chrome Trick again.

• The stovetop is often the most noticeably disgusting part of the kitchen, even in the homes of otherwise mostly neat people. Use your sponge and wipe it down. You don't have time to scrub the burned-on stuff, obviously, but you can easily remove all the black crusty bits, and every little bit helps.

• They'll probably need to throw something away eventually (a napkin, a paper cup, a phone number). Empty the garbage, if it overfloweth.

- Use your glass cleaner and a damp sponge to wipe the cabinet fronts. You'd be amazed at how much dirt and drippy crap is probably clinging to your cabinet fronts this very minute, and how big a difference it makes when they are cleaned.

You have now accomplished a thorough wipe-down/spruce-up, and your guests will probably be a little late. Wash your hands, check your reflection, and put on some music and/or lipstick. Dim as many lamps and light as many candles as you decently can. Fix yourself a drink. Put out a bowl of pretzels. Sit down for the first time in forty-five minutes and breathe deeply. Savor the whiff of ammonia.

10.

How to Hold Your Liquor

Why You Should Learn This

Every night, at parties and bars in every town across our great nation of drinkers, somebody somewhere gets sloppy. You've probably seen this person. If the sloppy person is a woman, you will have seen her stumbling intently across the room with mascara and lipstick smudged, holding her shoes in one hand, chain-smoking with the other, and looking for her friends, who have probably already left. If the sloppy person in question is a man, he may have made an inappropriate gesture or remark because he has lost control of his faculties and better sense, and he's either alone and trying to get the bartender to talk to him or he's in a fight outside.

You don't want to be that person.

We've been taught that outrageous, out-of-control drunkenness is funny, that it gets your attention or at least makes a great story. Women in particular seem to have been taught that obvious drunkenness is something men think is cute or attractive. But let's examine that premise more closely.

Things That *Are Cute or Attractive*	Things That *Are Not Cute or Attractive*
Bunnies	Vomit
Kittens	Slackened facial musculature
The sparkle in the eye of a witty conversationalist	Maudlin, slurred confessionals
"I'm so smart and interesting that every comment that drops from my lips is like a beautiful cultured pearl."	"I'm so drunk."

Clearly, there are numerous advantages to training your body to alert you when the state of sloppiness is imminent, in order to head it off at the pass. This is the best part of being able to hold your liquor: You can enjoy yourself without looking like an idiot.

How To

Know the Rules of Good Drinking

Everyone's body responds to different kinds of alcohol differently, and one of the first steps to enjoying a buzz that makes you lively and gregarious instead of pushy and loud is to learn what types of liquor you can't tolerate and avoid them. Fortunately, there are several good drinking ground rules that may help you avoid a lengthy, costly, embarrassing trial-and-error process.

• Stay away from novelty shots and drinks with stupid names. Ordering them is funny only once.

• Always drink the best beer, wine, or liquor you can afford. That's not just good drinking, that's good living: There's no point in settling for garbage just to get drunk.

• It's not conventional wisdom for nothing: The quickest way to get ugly, sloppy drunk is to embrace an injudicious *variety* of beverages in one night.

• Unless you're talking about sangria, big pieces of fruit do not belong in cocktails and, especially, in beers. There are relatively few exceptions to this rule: the maraschino cherry in a Manhattan, a Rob Roy, or an old-fashioned; the lime or lemon slice in many gin- and rum-based drinks like rickeys, caipirinhas, and Tom Collinses. Otherwise, fruit in a drink is a gateway to sloppiness. If you find yourself ordering rum drinks (common violators of the fruit rule) at a bar, that bar should be on the beach, or the drink recipe should be from Latin America. And if you have to put lemon or lime in a beer to make it drinkable, take that as a sign that the beer should not be drunk by you, or possibly by any human. (And yes, that means Corona. With the exception of weisses, real beers are not yellow.)

• There's no shame in drinking a tall glass of water before a night of drinking. This simple step can save you a world of pain later on.

Pick a Signature Drink

Pick a drink that appeals to you and stick to it. Master it. Learn all you can about it and make it the basis of your drinking repertoire. The reasons for doing this are many: Your body will more quickly recognize and adapt to it, and will come to absorb it in a way that will keep you in good conversational form and out of trouble. Your dates and friends will always know what to get you when they buy a round. Knowing how to mix a particular drink well or knowing a lot about, say, red wine, is also to your credit, as it gives you a specialty—you can never have too many specialties. If you like, consider changing your signature drink periodically, every nine months to a year. Here are some good signature drinks and guidelines for their usage.

Cocktails

Cocktails are the best signature drinks because they're easy to dilute (or strengthen) to varying degrees as your tolerance grows. The best ones also don't have stupid names, and you can always start slow.

- Scotch and soda. This is a classic drink, very light and refreshing.

- Whiskey and ginger ale, also known as a highball. Another classic drink for folks who like them a little on the sweet side. (If you like it a little less sweet, try a whiskey with equal parts club soda and ginger ale, also known as a Presbyterian.)

- Gimlet: gin or vodka. Sweet and tart. Gimlet glasses are also among the cooler-looking cocktail glasses around.

- Gin or vodka tonic. Old faithful.

Overrated Cocktails

- Whiskey and rum sours. A bit sticky, and the sugar tends to make you drunker and sloppier faster. Whiskey sours are not the burliest drinks to be seen holding either.

• Cosmopolitans. Tasty, to be sure, but also sloshy, and alarmingly expensive in most bars. In general, the more alcohol-derived ingredients there are in a drink, the less of them you will be able to drink in one night without risking loss of motor function (this includes the martini family, of which the cosmopolitan is a member, and tasty but dangerous drinks like Manhattans).

• Anything with orange juice in it. Orange juice is for breakfast.

Wine

Wine can be a great signature drink if you do most of your drinking at restaurants, parties, or upscale bars. It's best not to rely on most bars having a very good wine selection though, and ordering house wine will often get you treated and feeling like a chump. So be a wine drinker if you drink under controlled conditions.

Entire books have been written about the selection and enjoyment of wine, but here are some basics for the signature wine drinker:

• Pick a certain grape and make it yours, preferably one that's not as well trodden as a merlot or a Chardonnay: Be a pinot noir person, a syrah person, a red zinfandel person. Or pick one of the many wonderful non-French wine countries and become an honorary citizen: Australia, Spain, Argentina.

• Wine drinkers are often expected to know why they're drinking the wine they're drinking, so it's good to know a little bit about your wine, but not so much that you come off as a pedant. Make friends with your local wine merchants and have them tell you as much as they can about your specialty grape (they love doing this), then parrot shamelessly. No one will ever know.

• A note to the penurious: An extremely corpulent wine store owner I once met (the kind of fat man who offers unsolicited advice and is utterly, inexplicably worshiped by every dog and child within ten feet) told me that the difference between a $9 bottle of wine and a $12 bottle of wine is $3 worth of money and about $10 worth of quality and enjoyment.

Beer

Certain people in the employ of certain domestic beer-making companies—that is to say, advertising people—would have you believe that drinking microbrewery or foreign beer is anti-populist, elitist, something that only snobs and the hopelessly uncool would do. The thing to remember is that these people are being paid to tell you this.

How to Be a Good Signature Beer Drinker

• In general, beers that are mixed with fruits and chocolates—novelty beers—are not the kind of beers you want to make a habit of drinking.

• Beer is really seasonal, like most things made from natural ingredients: creamy, thick, dark beers like stouts and porters are great winter beers; golden beers like weisses and pale ales are best in summer. Weisses, in particular, are the white shoes of the beer world: They're best between Memorial Day and Labor Day.

• Never be a signature "light beer" drinker. If you're worried about putting on weight as a result of drinking too much beer, for God's sake, address it in some other way. Switch to wine for a while, drink less of a more complicated brew, or get yourself to the gym.

Know Your Tipping Point

The tipping point is the point at which further drinking becomes inadvisable and you need to slow down or stop altogether. The good news is this: If you're worried about getting a reputation as a lightweight, the fact is nobody really notices when anyone else stops drinking, unless attention is foolishly called to it. Unless you actually say, "Whoa, I'd better slow down, har har," nobody will even see that you've been holding the same glass for twenty minutes without drinking from it.

The bad news is that for some, the tipping point is as elusive as the yeti. Some ways to keep track of your own inebriation, if that's commonly a struggle for you:

• Go to the bathroom every hour or so, even if you don't have to actually use it, and take note of whether your ears are ringing, the toilet paper holder is unusually fascinating, or you're having a hard time handling soap.

• Count. Count your drinks. Simple, but nobody does it. If you get to a prime number above five, you should probably stop.

• Observe the person in your company that you admire most, and make sure that person is always one drink ahead of you. This may seem a little mercenary, and in a way it is. You are co-opting the strength of his or her liver. But it never hurts to have a mentor. And if you manage to pass your tipping point, keep that one person you admire in view and make sure you are never talking louder, talking more, or wearing less clothing than that person is.

• Ask yourself: "What would Humphrey Bogart and/or Lauren Bacall do?" You could do a lot worse than to keep these two at the back of your mind as last-resort behavior consultants; career drinkers and high livers who nevertheless wouldn't have been caught dead "just lying down for a minute" in a public place or yelling "woo!" on a dance floor.

11.

————————

How to Cure a Hangover

Why You Should Learn This

Some hangovers are better than others. If you can sit on the couch all day watching football and/or E!, moving as little as possible, grunting with pain, and eating tiny tiny pieces of some inoffensive carbohydrates to soak up all the terrible things in your stomach, well, that hardly even counts as a hangover. You were spared. You were one of the lucky ones; you didn't have to learn the meaning of real pain. When you have to be a functional victim—when you have to move, or help your parents, or teach an English as a Second Language class, or go to work—that's when you know what a real hangover's all about. When you'd shave all your hair off if somebody promised you it would help. Because your hair hurts anyway. That's when you need a scientific cure for your hangover.

How To

When you have a hangover, you feel as if you're dying, but the real problems are:

• You have toxins (congeners from the booze and acetaldehyde from your body's processing of alcohol) running amok in your system.

• You're dehydrated.

• Alcohol tends to fry up or render useless any helpful vitamins or minerals that you may have had stored up in your body, which means there's nothing to stop the toxins from doing whatever they want to you.

The quickest and least painful way to alleviate these problems follows.

1. Start addressing the hangover the night before. Before you pass out, if you come home drunk you should drink a really unpleasant amount of nonalcoholic fluid and take a multivitamin. Some people say drink a glass of water for every glass of alcohol you consumed. We all know that's impossible. Suck down two or three tall glasses and that's probably about the best you can do. If the thought of water is gross, try a lower-acid juice like white grape juice or apple juice, or buy a couple of sports drinks (foul as they are) on the way home and drink them both. What you really want is fluid *and* electrolytes; get them before it's too late and while you're in a guzzling frame of mind, because tomorrow morning the last thing you'll want to do is put more fluid in your stomach. Also, make sure you go to the bathroom before bed.

Whatever you do, remember this: No pain relievers, no acetaminophen. Contrary to popular belief, these will aggravate your symptoms rather than preempt them and make it harder for your liver to do its job, which is process a lot of toxins while you're passed out.

2. The morning of, begin helping your body detoxify. When you get up, take a vitamin C tablet and a vitamin B tablet—this is in addition to the multi the night before. You need antioxidants that will get to work beating back the alcohol by-products in your body. Take these pills with sips—not gulps—of two parts orange juice diluted with one part water. Here's why I say sip:

3. Do not guzzle fluids the morning of a hangover. Yes, you're dehydrated. Yes, you're thirsty and you want to get some fluids into your body. But it doesn't follow that gulping a big glass of water will make you feel better. A stomach full of nasty juices diluted with ten ounces of water will just make you feel sloshy and terrible, and you may end up horking, which will leave you even more dehydrated than before. So instead of gulping, exercise all your powers of self-restraint and sip. Pour yourself three beverages:

- One tall glass of two parts orange juice diluted with one part water, as above.

- One tall glass of regular water.

- A tall, thick smoothie containing strawberries (at least five), a couple of cups of cold milk or soy milk, a half cup of orange juice, a banana, and a handful of blueberries. Beg somebody to go get this for you or make it yourself in a blender. This is a powerful stew of antioxidants, carbohydrates, potassium, and stomach-calming dairy that will start to counteract all the bad juju in your body.

Every two minutes, take a sip from one of these three beverages in turn. It should take you a while to finish all three. That's fine. By the end of it you'll be on your way to rehydration without feeling watery and sloshy.

4. Eat tiny bites of carbohydrates. Find yourself some crackers, white bread, or a plain bagel with nothing on it and eat small chunks every two minutes or so throughout the morning. These bits of solid food will help provide some needed energy and give your stomach something spongy and nonacidic to work on.

5. Take two aspirins. Now's the time for those pain relievers, if you've got them. And you'll probably need them.

Skills That Save Your Butt,
or Someone Else's

12.

How to Do the Heimlich Maneuver

Why You Should Learn This

If you're lucky, you will never have to use this skill at all. Nobody ever wants to be called upon to do the Heimlich maneuver, and nobody's likely to ask you to demonstrate your technique just for a larf. It's the kind of thing you shouldn't walk out of the house without knowing, however, because you could save someone's life.

How To

Before you do anything:

1. Ask if the victim if he or she can speak,

and

2. Have someone call 911 immediately.

Doing the Heimlich on someone who isn't actually chok-ing is dangerous. That said, if someone is clearly struggling to breathe, don't wait to figure out whether or not it's legit. Call 911. If the person cannot speak, perform the Heimlich. If the person can, he or she isn't choking, although it may still be an emergency.

If the victim is still conscious:

1. Stand behind the victim.

2. Put your arms around his or her upper abdomen.

3. Make a fist with one hand at the bottom of the breast-bone. Make sure your fist is actually below the breastbone, however, or you might break the victim's sternum while you're trying to save his or her life.

4. Cup your fist firmly in your other hand.

5. With your cupped hand, push your fist upward and in-ward in one strong, quick movement. If you just push up-ward, all you're doing is creating pressure on the sternum. What you want is to push pressure up into the chest and lungs behind the sternum. So aim up *and* slightly in.

6. Repeat until the windpipe is cleared, using strong, deliberate, separate movements (don't be too gentle—your arms should hurt the next day), about one push every second. Do not stop until the windpipe is cleared.

If the victim loses consciousness or is unconscious when you begin:

1. Lay the victim down on his or her back.

2. Straddle the victim's legs so that you're facing his or her chest.

3. Put the heel of your hand on the middle abdomen, fingers pointing up toward the ceiling. Again, don't place your hand too close to the breastbone or you will impact it when you push.

4. Reinforce your hand by placing the other hand over it.

5. Push upward toward the victim's chin with the heel of your bottom hand, using a strong, firm, deliberate movement.

6. Repeat until the windpipe is cleared or the victim regains consciousness.

If you clear the windpipe, but the victim is still unconscious and doesn't appear to be breathing:

1. Kneel near the victim's head.

2. Tilt the head to the side, open the mouth, and with your fingers, clear his or her mouth of whatever was obstructing the windpipe.

3. Tilt the head so that the chin is pointing up.

4. Put your ear next to the victim's mouth and listen carefully for breathing, watching the chest for any sign of rising and falling.

5. If you don't detect any breathing whatsoever, you must do artificial respiration. Put one hand under the victim's neck to support it, and with the other hand pinch his or her nostrils closed.

6. Take a deep, deep breath.

7. Cover the victim's mouth with your own, creating an airtight seal. In other words you want to place your lips just outside of the victim's.

8. Breathe into the mouth until you see the victim's chest expand. This may take several breaths in a row. If you do not see the chest expand or cannot force air into the victim's lungs, the windpipe hasn't been cleared, and you need to perform the Heimlich again. If you do see the chest expand, watch for an exhale.

9. Repeat every five seconds until you can see that the person is breathing again, or until help arrives.

CPR is different from the Heimlich and artificial respiration: It requires formal training and can be dangerous if you do it incorrectly. Sign up today for a CPR training course—it's a couple of hours out of your life but absolutely worth it.

13.

How to Use a Compass

Why You Should Learn This

Any skill that helps you out of a potential scrape is a good one to acquire, and being hopelessly lost certainly qualifies as a scrape. Likewise, any skill that's taught by the Boy Scouts and Girl Scouts is one to keep on a mental list of Good Stuff to Know. (Including "how to raise money for recreational trips by selling merchandise door-to-door.") What we're talking about are basic survival skills, the kind of stuff that helps you make it out of the woods alive. You could do a lot worse than to dig up your old Boy Scout or Girl Scout handbook and actually learn all the things that you were too busy fishing or selling cookies to bother with when you were ten—a well-trained scout is a serious badass. In the meantime, or if you've already lost that ancient handbook, one of the easiest survival skills is learning to use a compass.

How To

While traveling on foot cross-country, you can keep yourself from getting lost in one of two ways:

1. Have a map and know where you are on the map at all times.

2. Travel without a map but know what direction you want to go at all times.

A compass is essential in either case. Your basic magnetic compass can be used with or without a topographical map and has five important features:

• Direction-of-travel arrow (this is usually printed or etched on the plastic)

• Compass needle (this moves on its own so that it is always pointing at magnetic north)

• Compass housing, or bezel (this has degrees printed all the way around it and you can rotate it with your fingers)

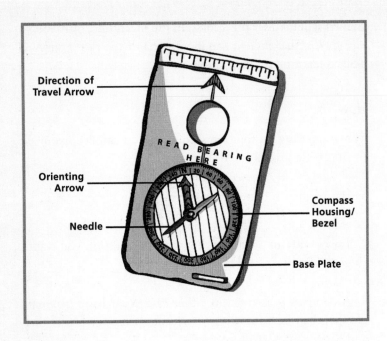

Direction of Travel Arrow

READ BEARING HERE

Orienting Arrow

Needle

Compass Housing/ Bezel

Base Plate

• Orienting arrow (this points to the spot on the compass housing marked 360 degrees, or N, and moves as you rotate the housing)

• Base plate

Using a Compass with a Topographical Map

1. Know what your topographical map and your compass do not have in common. Topographical maps (as opposed to,

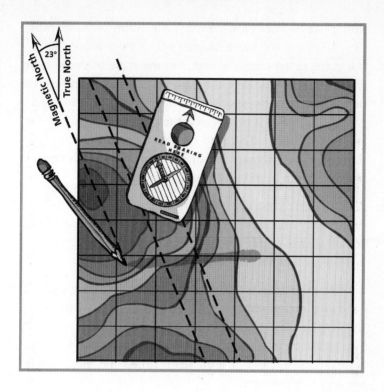

say, your road atlas) are the kind hikers use, and they denote various altitudes and landmarks in a particular region, as well as something called the angle of declination in that region. The angle of declination is, simply, the difference between magnetic north and true north (you know that magnetic north isn't actually the north pole, right?), which changes from place to place cross-country, depending on how strong the pull of the Big Earth Magnet is in a given locale. We're not going to get technical here, but the angle of declination is important if you use a compass, because your compass is nothing more or less spooky and magical than a little needle with a magnet on it that detects the gravitational pull of the Big Earth Magnet. That is to say, your compass needle thinks north is magnetic north, but your map thinks north is true north—as in the geographic north pole.

2. Find where your map says magnetic north is. This will probably be expressed on your map as degrees (east or west), as well as with a little arrow pointing somewhere left or right of geographic north.

3. Make your map and compass speak the same language. Line up a straight-edge over that magnetic north arrow on the map, and use a pencil to draw a magnetic north-south line across the map. In fact, you may find it helpful to draw several parallel lines across the map at the same angle. You'll see why in a moment.

4. Hold the map and compass out in front of you so that they're both parallel to the ground.

5. Place your compass on the map with the long edge of the base plate connecting where you are now with where you want to go (this means the direction-of-travel arrow will be pointing at your destination on the map).

6. Keeping the compass where it is on the page, turn the housing or bezel until the orienting arrow is parallel to the magnetic north-south line you drew on the map. Keep in mind you're interested in aligning with magnetic north on the map, so what you *don't* want to do is rotate the housing until the orienting arrow covers the compass needle, which will be pointing to where magnetic north is in the real world from wherever you're standing. If you drew several parallel lines across the page at the angle of declination, it'll be much easier to get your orienting arrow lined up just by eyeballing the closest one.

7. Standing in place and holding the compass still, turn your body until the magnetic compass needle is right over the orienting arrow.

8. At this point, the direction-of-travel arrow is pointing at your destination. Walk in that direction while keeping the magnetic needle over the orienting arrow. It's often helpful to pick a landmark in the right direction, walk to it, then pick another landmark past that one in the right direction and walk to it, and so on.

Using a Compass Without a Map

1. Know where you're going, or know where you've been. A compass is all you need to get to someplace and back again without getting lost, which makes it ideal for a rambling day hike cross-country. If you say at the beginning of the day, "Hey, let's just hike and see what we find," you can use the compass as described below to make sure you don't accidentally wander off course. If you use a compass to keep track of the direction you're heading, you can simply reverse your bearing at the end of the day and know exactly how to get back to where you started.

2. Aim the direction-of-travel arrow in the direction you want to go.

3. Rotate the housing until the compass needle points to N or 360 degrees.

4. Walk in your chosen direction, keeping the compass needle steady at 360 degrees.

5. Note your bearing. Your bearing is the degree that touches the direction-of-travel arrow—usually there's a little pointer that says "read bearing here."

6. To get back to where you started:

• Rotate the housing halfway around, or 180 degrees in either direction.

• Rotate your body until the compass needle points to 360 again.

• Walk where the direction-of-travel arrow is pointing.

Troubleshooting

I want to keep walking east (or west or northwest or whatever) but there's a big lake (or rock or marshland or whatever) I have to get around. What do I do? Pick a direction to walk around the obstacle—to the left or the right—and turn your body 45 degrees in that direction (watch the compass). Follow your new bearing, keeping the needle steady and counting every time your left foot hits the ground, until you've passed the obstacle. Then turn 90 degrees in the other direction and walk the same number of paces. When you've finished your paces, turn 45 degrees in the same direction you turned to walk around the obstacle. (So if you turned 45 degrees left then 90 degrees right, you'll turn 45 degrees left again when you're past the obstacle.)

All that said, if you've got a *map* and you plotted a course right through a lake you're not using your head. The shortest distance between two points may be a straight line, but not if there's a something big along that line that you have to navigate around. Use the 45-90-45-degree trick to get around smallish things that crop up on your path, but if there's a lake or a marsh or something equally big and unwalkable between you and your destination, do your hike in two parts: plot a course that skirts the obstacle at an angle, then angle back to your destination. Depending on how big the lake or whatever is, this will probably save you time compared to walking up to it and then around it.

What if I'm hiking with a compass and no map and I don't want to travel in one direction all day? Don't go switching your bearing too often because that's a really good way to get lost. But if you walked due east for about two hours at a steady pace, then decided to walk north of that for an hour and then turn back, you can walk south for an hour and then due west for two hours—that is, walk in reverse along each of your bearings for as long as you followed each bearing. A good idea is to have a little pad and a pencil with you to keep a log of your bearings, and note what the time was each time you changed direction.

14.

How to Change a Flat Tire

Why You Should Learn This

There's no reason not to learn how to change a flat tire, unless you're accompanied everywhere by a mechanic, or have an entourage of toadies eager to do your dirty work. *Learning* how to change a flat tire is a piece of cake. It's actually *doing* it that sucks.

The steps that follow are going to sound deceptively simple. That's because they are—emphasis on *deceptively.* So many things can and do go wrong when you need to change a flat tire that some of our wiser ancestors invented AAA. There are some times when you shouldn't (or really won't want to) attempt to change a flat tire on your own, and should call in the professionals:

- If it's after dark.

- If it's raining or snowing.

- If the road you're stranded on has an up- or downgrade (you'll need to be towed to a flat spot).

- If you don't have a jack, lug wrench, and/or spare tire, and you left your magic wand at home.

Of course, you could go your whole life calling for roadside assistance when you get a flat tire . . . that's kind of what they're hoping you'll do. But if you have no cell phone, are strapped for cash, or aren't a member of any roadside assistance program through your car insurance, AAA, or something like it (are you *crazy*?), it's good to know how to change a flat tire yourself. Of course, knowing how to do it is no guarantee that the experience won't still suck.

How To

Know the Right Place and Time to Change a Flat

Right	Wrong
a flat road	a hill (don't try to jack a car up on a hill—like, ever)

open road, clear sightlines	a curve in the road that makes it difficult for oncoming drivers to see you
not too much traffic	a busy street at rush hour
in daylight or under a streetlamp	after dark, in the dark
in good weather	in rain or a snowstorm

Get to the Side of the Road Safely

Whether you realize that you have a flat because you're listing to one side and wobbling, or because you actually hear the tire blow out, don't slam on the brakes. Slow down gradually, and pull over to the side of the road as soon as you can—don't drive for miles looking for a good spot if you can avoid it, or you'll have to replace the rim as well as the tire. That costs lots of money. You probably don't have it. Just get over.

Make the Car Safe on the Road

• Turn on your hazards.

• If you have an automatic, put it in park; if it's manual, put it in first or second gear.

- Turn off the ignition.

- Put on the emergency brake.

Assemble Your Weapons

To change a flat tire, you must have these three things:

- A spare tire

- A jack

- A lug wrench that fits your wheel's lug nuts

"Lug wrench? Hmmwha?" you say. "If I had a spare tire, would I know it, necessarily? Is it possible that these things are in my trunk right now and I'm not aware of them?" Assuming you are not reading this by the side of the road (or even if you are), go to your trunk, right now, bringing this book. Open your trunk. There's usually a compartment under the floor—look under the carpeting . . . See a big round thing? That's your spare tire, or more accurately, your spare wheel (a rubber tire that's not attached to a metal rim isn't much use to you, unless you know how to mount tires). Does the tire look sturdy and inflated? Is the rubber free of cracks and splits? If you give it a rap with your knuckles does it hurt a little? If so, the tire is probably holding air and you're probably good to go—although unfortunately, you won't know

this for sure until you've put it on the car. If your spare tire looks flat, cracked, damaged, or is totally not there at all, invest in a new one ASAP.

Now look for your jack. Play with it for a moment and figure out what makes it work. Most jacks work by sticking the handle into a socket on the body of the jack, and turning the handle.

Now look for a lug wrench. (Sometimes the lug wrench is actually part of the jack handle; look for something that is long and metal and has a rounded end.) Boy oh boy is it important that your lug wrench fits your lug nuts. Most of the time it will—that's why it's in your trunk and not somebody else's. But if you've got a used car that's passed through several owners, some of them with MacGyver tendencies, you may be holding a lug wrench that somebody figured they could "make work when the time came." MacGyver: smartypants. People who believe in improvisational lug wrenches: not so smart. While you're out there at the car, you may want to check to make sure your lug wrench works for your lug nuts, using steps 6 and 7 below.

If you don't have all three of the necessary pieces of equipment, it's time to get on the cell phone or start hoofing it to a pay phone or gas station. (Whatever you do, don't accept a lift from anybody who's not in a uniform or driving a tow truck.) If you do have the necessary equipment, take it all out of the trunk and put it on the ground next to the flat tire.

There are some other pieces of equipment that are so very useful to changing a flat tire that one hesitates to call them "optional," but in a pinch you could do without them:

- A screwdriver (preferably flat-head)

- A big, nonpointy rock, a brick, a wheel chock, or a 6-inch-long two-by-four. (You could actually have one of these cut for you at a lumber store in about five minutes, and just keep it in the trunk. That's a hint.)

- A blanket or drop cloth

- WD-40 or similar lubricant

And if you're like some of my friends, you also have wet-naps in the car to clean your hands afterward. Let us now praise famous wetnaps.

Changing the Tire

1. Figure out where to place the jack. Most cars have a couple of different reinforced spots on the frame that can bear the weight of the car when it's jacked up. Your owner's manual will tell you where those spots are, and you'll want to jack up your car at whichever one of those spots is closest to the flat tire. Scooch around under the car until you can actually see the spot that the owner's manual is referring to.

What you're looking for is a slot or notch that looks like it corresponds to some part of your jack. When you find it, put your jack on the ground under the reinforced spot (don't jack up the car yet). If you don't have your owner's manual, here are some good places to look:

- On the frame about 8 inches behind the front wheel

- On the frame about 8 inches away from the front or back bumper

- On the frame about 8 inches in front of the rear tire

There are a couple of really bad places to jack up your car:

- The front bumper

- The back bumper

- Anywhere on the body of the car (usually painted), as opposed to the frame itself (usually not)

In any event, you'll know if you've chosen the wrong spot to jack up your car by the horrible groaning and creaking sounds your car's body will make as it crumples.

2. Remove the hubcap. This is where that flathead screwdriver comes in handy. Slide the screwdriver under the hubcap to pop it off. Some lug wrenches or jack handles have a

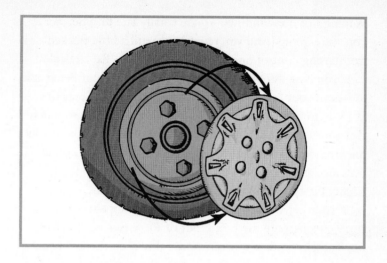

flat end for this express purpose, and some hubcaps have little notches along the rim, likewise for this express purpose. Keep your hubcap on the ground nearby; it's a good place to store removed lug nuts.

3. Loosen the lug nuts. Oh yeah. This is where the party starts. Right. Now.

Your lug nuts are the four or five knobby-looking things that hold your tire on. At a service station or garage, lug nuts get taken off and put back on with hydraulic tools. All you've got is a funny-looking wrench. Cars are whizzing by you, possibly honking, possibly with angrily waved fists coming out the windows. You're totally late to wherever you were going. And you're probably still a little freaked out from losing control on the road. Changing a flat tire rules!

If you have WD-40, you have a better chance of being able to loosen your lug nuts without losing your cool. Spray the WD-40 to help lubricate the lug nuts, but don't use so much that your wrench will slip right off as well. Then pick up your lug wrench and make sure the round end fits over your lug nuts nice and snug. Now try turning the wrench to the left (righty tighty, lefty loosey). It will probably be hard to do.

If your lug wrench has a crossbar (and hopefully it does, since crossbars are the best kinds of lug wrenches), orient it horizontally so that you can stomp down on the left-hand side, or wham it with a rock. Get the nuts loosened however you can, but be safe. Usually it's easier to loosen the nuts alternately—that is, loosen one then skip one, loosen one then skip one. (If you have four lug nuts, loosen them in alternating order: one, three, two, four.) Keep going till you've got each of the lug nuts loosened so much that two or three more turns by hand should be enough to remove them completely.

4. Reinforce the opposite wheel. Wedge a nonpointy rock or piece of wood behind the wheel opposite your flat tire. It will probably need some reinforcement when you start jacking the car up.

5. Jack the car up slightly.

- You'll probably need to scootch under the car again (here's where the drop cloth comes in handy for preserving your clothes) to find the notch, groove, or slot.

- Crank the jack up until it's almost touching the car.

- Get the top of the jack oriented in the right place.

- Get back out from under the car as much as possible and work the jack handle.

You don't want to jack the tire completely off the ground at this point, or the wheel will spin while you're trying to remove the lug nuts the rest of the way. Jack the car up just enough that the flat tire is still touching the pavement a bit.

6. Remove the lug nuts. It may be helpful to remove the bottom ones first, or remove them in alternate order, because the tire may start to tilt or slide out as you remove the lug nuts. Put the lug nuts in your hubcap for safekeeping.

7. Slide, jimmy, or haul the wheel off (as opposed to trying to get the flat tire itself off the wheel. That may be obvious to you, but just to be crystal clear here . . .). Put it aside.

8. Jack the car up a bit more. You want the car up just high enough to be able to put on the fully inflated spare tire—no need to jack it up higher than is absolutely necessary.

9. Put on the spare. Align the holes in the wheel with the threaded shafts, and slide the spare on, pushing it all the way back. Note whether there is a speed limit indicated on your spare tire—especially if you have one of the compressed "doughnut" models.

10. Screw the lug nuts back on in alternating order.

11. Lower the jack. If your spare tire isn't holding air, you'll know soon after lowering the car back down onto the ground.

12. Tighten the lug nuts, again in alternating order. Use all your strength to do this; you don't want the spare tire to spin right off.

13. Put everything away in the trunk: the tools, the flat tire, the jack, the drop cloth. Now's the time for that wetnap, if you've got one.

14. Drive slowly to wherever you were going, keeping in mind that a spare tire isn't meant to be driven on for more than a day or two, and never at more than 55 miles per hour. Buy a replacement tire for your flat as soon as possible. And some more wetnaps.

15.

―――――――

How to Jump Start a Car

Why You Should Learn This

Because you want to be a roadside hero. Because "sort of" knowing how to do this can get you killed or damage your car. Because not knowing how to do it at all can get you sneered at by service station guys. Because sooner or later you're going to leave your headlights on.

How To

Jump starting a car is actually really easy, once you get past the fact that you must memorize how to do it. Doing steps out of order or not at all is a bad idea. Bad as in, "electrical sparks coming out of your engine."

1. Be safe. Get your car to a safe but noticeable spot, turn on the hazard lights, and get your jumper cables out of the trunk. It is a statistical fact that having a set of jumper cables in your trunk will increase the likelihood of being able to jump start your car by 100 percent. Don't rely on the kindness of strangers *and* the ability of strangers to be thoroughly equipped to solve your problems—at least, not at the same time.

2. Turn everything unnecessary off. Turn off the headlights, unplug the cell phone charger, turn off the dome light, don't have the A/C or heat set to run, and turn off the hazard lights once you've gotten help. All these things create an electrical drain on the battery while it's trying to absorb much-needed juice.

3. Find the battery. Pop your hood, prop it open, and look for your battery, which should be easy to find: It's a big black deep box that either has two metal terminals on top, or two terminal caps (one red, one black).

4. Check out the battery for three things:

  • If there are cracks in the battery casing and/or it's leaking anything, don't even try jump starting it; get to a service station and buy a new battery.

  • If there's corrosion on the battery terminals (white, yellow, or greenish), you should try to clean it off with a wire brush or scour pad.

• If it's really cold outside you should remove the vent caps (carefully) to see if the fluid inside the battery is frozen—all batteries are filled with an electrolyte solution (part water, part sulfuric acid), and in weak batteries this fluid can freeze at about 15 to 20 degrees Fahrenheit. If you see ice crystals in the battery fluid, don't try to jump the car. You have to thaw the battery fluid first; get the car into a warm garage and wait. In cold cities people often plug their cars into engine heaters overnight to keep their battery fluid from freezing, and if you're in a jam, it may be worth your while to see if any of your neighbors have one. As a last resort, some folks have been known to remove the entire battery, bring it into the house, and put it into a tub of lukewarm water for an hour. My own father used to go out into the driveway with an extension cord and a carefully wielded hair dryer at 6 A.M. on cold school days in Chicago. But by his own admission, that's a little nuts.

5. Attract a do-gooder whose car actually started that day. Frequently, attracting a do-gooder is as simple as following steps 1 through 4 above: There's a certain, magnificent kind of person who just can't resist the sight of somebody monkeying under the hood of a car with its hazards on.

6. Get the cars into position. Ask the do-gooder to pull his or her car as close as possible to yours *without* touching it.

7. Take a look at your battery. See how the red battery head is labeled "positive" and the black one "negative"? That's important. Memorize this phrase: *Red is always positive; black is always negative.*

8. The mantra of the jump-starter: Here's the next thing to memorize—even if you pay attention to nothing else:

red for me

red for you

black for you

block for me

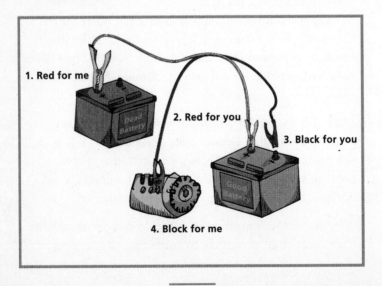

Got that? That's basic shorthand for how to attach the cables and in what order:

- Attach one red cable to your positive battery terminal

- Attach the other red end to their positive terminal.

- Then attach one black cable to their negative terminal.

- Clamp the other end to the unpainted frame or a metal part of the engine block of your car. Don't attach the cable to your negative terminal, and don't attach it to the frame anywhere near your battery. This end of the cable grounds the flow of electricity.

9. Ask the do-gooder to start his or her car. You should stand back (and definitely don't smoke or light a match) while this is done. Let the do-gooder rev their engine gently.

10. Wait a minute or two.

11. Try starting the dead car. (No need to disconnect anything yet.) If it doesn't start, wait a few more minutes, and give it one or two more tries, but don't go pumping away at the ignition for more than thirty seconds.

If the dead car doesn't start after five minutes of transferring juice from the live car, it's probably not going to start at all, and you need to get to a service station. If it does start:

12. Keep the newly resurrected car engine running while you remove the cables in *reverse* order: block, black, your red, my red. Got that? Block, black, your red, my red.

13. Thank the do-gooder—graciously and genuinely.

14. Drive your car around for at least fifteen minutes afterward (thirty minutes is better) to give the battery a chance to recharge; don't turn the car off for at least half an hour or you'll be repeating this whole process later in the day. Every time you have to jump start your battery, you weaken it, so you don't want to make a habit of this, even though you can be justifiably proud of jumping your car successfully.

Now go out there and *be* a do-gooder.

Skills That
Make You (Feel) Cooler

16.

How to Open a Champagne Bottle

Why You Should Learn This

Outside of pennant-winning clubhouses, most people are secretly afraid to take the responsibility of opening a bottle of
anything that's both volatile *and* expensive. And for good reason: They might break something; they might lose an eye;
they might spill or shake the precious golden liquid; they
might fail. Which makes you a hero for volunteering when
the inevitable question, "Does anybody know how to open
this?," arises. Also, as the bottle opener, you are at the festive
center of activity, and not one of the hapless schlubs standing
to one side with glass in hand, trying not to look too eager,
or too anxious that the bottle will run out before their glass is
filled.

Most of the people who *aren't* secretly afraid to open a champagne bottle think the best method is to put two thumbs to the base of the cork, push up, and pray. Those people account for the majority of the world's many champagne-related injuries.

It's possible to open a champagne bottle safely, festively, and considerately, without sacrificing any of the fun or overall specialness of the moment. When you're opening champagne, it pays to remember the specialness is in the bottle, not in your thumbs. Unlike most of the rest of life.

How To

1. Get a towel. If the occasion is the least bit fussy or fancy, and most champagne-related occasions are, there should be a clean kitchen towel at hand, and it's better to use it, especially if the champagne bottle is wet or slippery from being chilled (either on its side in the fridge for an hour, or in ice, cork side up, for twenty minutes). If you're at the kind of party where asking for a towel is liable to brand you a fussy, fancy sort yourself, then skip it.

2. Remove the hood. The hood is the wire jobby that appears, falsely, to keep the cork in. Pull the wire loop toward you, then twist it (righty tighty, lefty loosey) till the bottom of the hood has widened enough to liberate the bottle.

3. Remove the foil. There's some inconsistency surrounding the issue of whether it's really necessary to remove all the foil, or just the foil covering the cork and the bottle's mouth. But foil is shiny and sparkly and, hell, why waste precious drinking time taking it all off.

4. Angle the bottle away from you, and away from anybody else. Most people do this by resting the base of the bottle on their stomach or hip. This is acceptable—just don't tuck the bottle into your armpit.

5. Begin wrestling with the cork.

If you have a towel: Cover and hold the cork with one end of the towel, and use the other end to help you get a firm grip on the bottom part of the bottle's neck—the shoulder, if you will. Using the cloth for resistance, gently begin twisting the bottle. As you twist, think with pity of anyone trying to do this without a towel. The cloth will at once make the twisting motion easier and will keep the cork from flying across the room when it pops out. Use your lucky towel to present the open bottle with a gallant flourish.

If you don't have a towel: Grasp the cork in one hand and take a firm grip on the bottle's neck with the other hand. Twist the bottle while holding the cork still. The foil at the bottle's neck should help provide some resistance, if you had the foresight and/or impatience to keep from tearing it all off. You will need to be aware of when the cork has been eased up a quarter of an inch or so—at this point, just a touch more leverage should result in the satisfying pop you seek. To ensure that the cork's pop doesn't accompany a swift short flight across the room into somebody's head, place your palm over the top of the cork, wrap your fingers around it, and rather than twisting, wiggle the cork side to side slightly until it poofs out of the bottle and into the palm of your hand, followed by a whiff of white mist. Toss the cork in the air and catch it behind your back, then take a bow.

6. Try not to gloat if you are lucky enough to be asked to pour too. Remember to tip the champagne flutes at a 45-degree angle as you pour down the side, so as not to dispense three inches of foam to the poor schlub who hid in the corner until it was safe to emerge with his glass.

17.

How to Send a Drink to Someone's Table

Why You Should Learn This

Sending a drink to someone's table is a classic gesture of flirtation and appreciation that never loses its charm or goes out of fashion. Who doesn't like being the object of some courteous, flattering attention? Who doesn't respect an admirer who puts his or her money where his or her mouth would like to be?

That said, no one can promise that everybody you'd like to buy a drink for will actually want one, or want one from you anyway. There are no guarantees of success. But if you make the gesture in the right spirit and with the right attitude, it's pretty close to irresistible. That is, if you're even remotely attractive.

How To

Sending a drink to someone's table is a little different from buying someone a drink at a bar—the rules are different and the expectations are different; it's a move from a whole different decade. It's a little more smooth.

When you buy someone a drink at a bar (or anyplace where there are no tables, or table service), a couple of rules apply. Usually, you should talk to the person first and ask if you can buy him or her a drink. If you're a guy, you have to be batting in the same league as your intended, if you get my drift, and you have to buy a drink for your intended's friend as well (and then direct your attention to the true object of your affection, so the friend doesn't get confused or salacious signals from you). If you're a woman, on the other hand, you will almost always get away with it no matter what league you're in, and you don't need to buy his or her friend a drink (it's a little cooler if you do, but beware: Some people will take it as an invitation to compete for your attention). It's a cruel world, but that's one of the perks of being a girl. Guys, don't feel too bad about it, there's always the glass ceiling— you may know it as a floor.

A bartender I spoke with recommended reading your server for cues when you order a drink for someone. A good bartender will let you know, in a sensitive fashion, whether you're wasting your time. If you say, "I'd like to buy drinks for these two ladies please, Sharlene," and Sharlene responds with a suspiciously toneless "Good luck," you are probably not the first to have dared to live recklessly and buy fruitlessly, or Sharlene has overheard the ladies talking about their still-active significant others and knows it's a lost cause.

Sending a drink to a person's table, on the other hand, obeys a different logic. Whether the table is at a bar, a club, or a restaurant (and whether or not you are likewise seated at a table), the procedure is as follows:

1. You don't have to talk to the person first. In fact, it's better if you don't. Think about it: Your intended is sitting at a table with friends. You walk over. You introduce yourself and announce your intention to buy him or her a drink, all the while standing awkwardly over the table, implicitly awaiting an invitation to sit down, which in turn makes your intended feel awkward, and as if she or he doesn't have a choice. Even if you are invited to sit, you still have to get the server's attention, and then wait for the drinks you promised to arrive—no, no, that won't do. That's too much time between cause and effect. That's much more embarrassing and presumptuous than you want to be. That's not smooth. You want to be cool. You want to be mysterious. You want to establish your admiration, and then leave the ball in your intended's court. The very existence of the table adds too much pressure to a first encounter in person: Basically, it's a shield for your intended if she or he doesn't like you.

2. You don't have to buy the person's friend a drink. Consider it above and beyond the call of duty. If you decide to do it anyway, note that it makes the server's job a little harder, and that you must be even more explicit than usual when you give him or her instructions. Which brings us to:

3. When you speak to the server, be explicit, humble, and charming. Get the server's attention and smile like the crush-stricken romantic loon that you are. Assume an attitude of hopeless enthusiasm (i.e., "I know it's crazy, but . . ." Except don't actually say that out loud). Say, "Hi, I'd like to send a drink to someone." Then point as subtly as you can to your intended while giving a very detailed description. "That beautiful/amazing/well-dressed guy/woman at the third table from the door, wearing the red sweater, with the black-framed glasses. Sitting next to the blonde. See him/her? Please let him/her know that the next drink is on me. My name is. . . . Thanks. Oh, and I'll have a scotch and soda please." *Always* order a drink for yourself as well so you can tip the server (generously) no matter what happens.

The server probably will not expect the tip from you right that minute, though. He or she will go deliver the message and see how it's received first, so don't press money into his or her palm while you're making the request; it's sleazy. Similarly, don't put your arm around the server and draw him or her into a chummy conspiratorial huddle—

you're not in this together; the server is doing you a solid. Whether you're rejected or not depends more on your demeanor and personal attributes than on the server, who is just doing his or her job with a graceful favor thrown in. Again, we live in a cruel world.

4. The server makes your offer. If you're not already at a table of your own, stand or sit in a clearly visible spot, preferably at some distance (diagonally across the room is ideal), to watch the whole thing go down. At this point, the offer will be conveyed to your intended by the server, who will probably say, "That person over there wants to buy your next drink, what are you having?" and point to you, so your intended can get a fair sense of the consequences of accepting your offer. You then have two options.

The straightforward way: When you're pointed to, simply nod and smile and try to look approachable, attractive, and harmless.

The sneak's way: Pretend that, having made the request, you're not keeping close track of whether or when it happens—read the menu, talk to a friend. Then glance over as if you're surprised to be pointed at, and nod in smooth, friendly recognition of what's taking place.

Of course, if it's a busy night the server may not be able to hop to your request immediately, so the sneak's way is your only option—when you feel like somebody's looking at you, it's probably the server pointing you out to your intended. Look over and act friendly.

5. Rejection or acceptance. Your intended actually has a choice. He or she can say, in flattered surprise, "Oh, um. Tell him/her thanks. I'm having a scotch and soda." Or she/ he can say, "Oh, um. Tell him/her no thanks, I'm okay." Because you're watching, you'll know as soon as the server turns around—if it's no go, you'll get a "Sorry, better luck next time" kind of grimace, or more humanely, the server will come to your table and deliver the bad news in person, preferably along with the drink that you ordered for yourself and that you will now drink in lonely solitude. Tip the server well anyway.

If it's a go, your server will simply turn around and go get your intended's order. Your intended will smile at you, and then you will smile back, and then you will cease eye contact and sit in your spot looking normal. This is *not* the moment to go over there. Repeat. Do not go over there yet.

6. The person's drink arrives. You may or may not be watching at the exact moment the drink arrives. But if you are, or if your intended catches your eye and smiles—and that's definitely what you're hoping will happen—smile back. Don't wink. Don't lift your glass and mouth, "To you, gorgeous," or "*Salut,* beautiful." Don't lift a silent meaningful toast. Just look normal and friendly. This is *still* not the moment to go over there.

7. Wait at least ten minutes to make contact. If you're having a good night, your intended will actually come speak to you, but if not, wait for the person to have a couple of sips of his or her drink and figure out what she or he would like to do. You need to sit still long enough for the server to come back to you and be paid and tipped for both your drinks—you definitely don't want the bill coming to the intended's table while you're at it. You also want to allow this time for the intended to be impressed by your restraint. A drink is not a ticket to your intended's table. It is a drink.

8. Pay for the drink and tip well.

9. If you definitely get a smile or a nod after some time has elapsed, go over and introduce yourself. Keep it simple. Say, "Hello, I'm Siobhan." (Except use your name . . . unless you think for some reason it will help to use mine.) Extend your hand and the person will introduce him- or herself and thank you for the drink. All you need to say is, "You're welcome. Do you mind if I join you for a moment?" The "for a moment" is key: You don't want your intended to feel cornered . . . even if you intend to sit next to them all night pitching woo, which you could very well do after this point. It's up to you. Go get 'em, tiger.

Troubleshooting

How do I know if it's a good idea to send a drink to someone? If the person is there with a date or someone who looks like they might be a date, it's totally inappropriate to send a drink. Other situations in which sending a drink is inappropriate or otherwise likely to flop:

• You are more than fifteen years older than your intended.

• Your intended is clearly at the bar, restaurant, or club for a special occasion—that is, his or her birthday, or a friend's birthday—where the "no thunder stealing" rule might be in effect.

• There's no table service at the bar, restaurant, or club.

• Your intended was just publicly dumped.

• Your intended looks mean.

• Your intended is not drinking anything. That is to say, wait for the person to order a first drink on their own, so you don't seem like a vulture, swooping down the minute somebody attractive walks through the door.

I sent over a drink and the person accepted it, but I didn't get a smile or any kind of friendliness in return. Now they've got their drink and they're drinking it and not looking at me and I don't know what to do. Do I go over there? No. That person, I'm sorry to say, is either rude or dumb. She or he doesn't want to be friends or anything else with you, but was rude enough to accept a drink from a stranger she or he has no intention of speaking to. Either that, or the person was dumb enough to think that accepting a drink from a stranger does not intimate any obligation to be friendly. Pick up the shattered pieces of your life and select a nicer target.

I sent over a drink and it was accepted, and later I went over and chatted the person up. But they seemed kind of frosty, or not my type. How much time should I spend trying to get this person to like me? You mean how much of a person's time does one drink buy you? To be honest, not much. If you're not hitting it off after fifteen minutes, or about as long as it took you to set up the transaction, excuse yourself politely and say, "Well, it was nice meeting you."

18.

How to Cook One "Signature Meal"

Why You Should Learn This

People who know how to cook really, really well are never lonely or bored. You will never see Julia Child at home on Saturday night alone with nothing to do. The Naked Chef, aka Jamie Oliver, has great parties and friends with neat haircuts. Emeril Lagasse has so much love to give they had to give him his own empire: He loves you; he loves everybody; he's in love with mankind—because it's great to be Emeril. All these people know that food is a tactile, sensual pleasure, and one of the best-known ways of endearing oneself to others. Everyone needs to eat, after all, and those who are hungry will gravitate toward nice food and the people who produce it. People who love food and know how to manipulate it beautifully are truly the blessed of the earth. It takes years of practice and trial and error and study and often several trips to France to join their ranks. Fortunately, however, it is easy to imitate them.

Knowing how to cook just one meal well is not only smart—it's also something you're likely to find quite useful. Women love men who can cook; men love women who can cook; women and men love women and men who can cook. If you can't cook, or don't like cooking, you have to be able to pretend you do or else no one will like you.

Consider the advantages of knowing how to make just one delicious, impressive-looking meal:

• People are always saying they love it when someone makes a candlelit dinner for them, and you'll know how to do that.

• You'll always have something to make if you're ever put on the spot. If someone you like comes over, for example, and you don't want them to leave, plying one's beloved with food is a timeless strategy. Or if you're ever invited to a potluck—yes, really, people still have those. Or if ravenous Visigoths take over your town.

• One great meal is usually enough to convince the unwitting and the generous that you're a great cook.

• It can, and should, be easy, but it looks hard, which makes you seem brilliant.

Now, lots of people like to cook and do it tolerably well, and this particular chapter is not for them: They should consult reputable cookbooks for a recipe that strikes their fancy, practice it, and commit it to memory. The simple suggestions that follow are really intended for the following kinds of readers:

1. People who don't like to cook

2. People who think they can't cook

3. People who don't like doing dishes and therefore do not cook

Recognizing that you are one of those three types is nothing to be ashamed of. All you have to do is learn how to make one signature meal.

How To

Important Tips for All Kinds of People Who Don't Cook

• The easiest cuisine to learn and do passably well is Italian. The Italians are on to something. They like to eat, they like to feel full, and their food has to be easy enough to make that everybody in the country has time to take a two-hour nap every afternoon. Hence pasta with vegetables. It's cheap, it's easy, and with a little bit of care and attention it tastes excellent.

• Here are some items to buy the next time you go to the grocery store, and to keep on hand: garlic, olive oil, linguine, quality grated parmesan cheese (the kind that doesn't come from a canister), some nice salad dressing, and butter (actual butter, not margarine or spread). These items play a significant role in the signature meal suggestion that follows, and are stock items in the pantry of someone who can't really cook but pretends to know how. Preparation is half the battle.

This meal is designed to serve two people. Meals for larger groups are probably best left to people who like to cook, but if you must, you can easily double the amounts and serve four. Serve with a bit of crunchy salad, a loaf of warmed-up bread, and a bottle of wine.

The Signature Meal of the Person Who Doesn't Like to Cook: Linguine with Broccoli Rabe and Garlic

This throws together in about fifteen minutes without much work, giving you more time to do other things, like flirt. If you've stocked up on the recommended pantry items, all you have to buy are the salad fixings, the broccoli rabe, and the wine. The meal also dirties a minimum amount of pots and pans.

1. Water: Put one large and one medium-sized pot of water on the stove to boil. While you're waiting, make your salad and put it in the fridge. When the water starts looking frisky (some small bubbles on the bottom, but not boiling yet) pour about 2 tablespoons of olive oil in a pan, swish it around to coat the bottom, and put the pan on low heat.

2. Garlic: Your garlic objective is to cut up three or four cloves into little garlic pieces and sauté them in hot olive oil until they get slightly crunchy and toast-brown. But garlic can be confusing—so tiny! So wrapped in inedible junk! What to do with it? Here's a handy tip for people boggled by garlic: Pull off a clove and put it on the counter. Rest the flat side of a wide-blade butter knife on top, and give the blade a little whap with the heel of your fist. This smooshes the clove a bit and loosens the skin, which you can then pull off and discard. Cut off the woody ends of the cloves, then slice each clove once lengthwise and about ten times widthwise. Now you are the garlic master. Cut up the garlic cloves, put them in the oil, and you're halfway there. Just stir every so often.

3. Broccoli rabe: Your broccoli rabe objective is tart, hassle-free, tender little chunks of greenery. Rinse two handfuls of broccoli rabe, squeeze the water out, and pat dry with a paper towel. Cut off the thick ends. Your water should be boiling at this point: gently slide the broccoli rabe into the medium-sized pot of boiling water for three minutes, then drain it thoroughly and set it aside.

4. Linguine: When your big pot of water starts boiling, make an O with your index finger and thumb: as much linguine as fits inside should be enough for two. To minimize awkward slurping while still affording satisfyingly twirlable pasta, break the dry linguine in half before putting it in the water.

5. Bread: Wrap the loaf in tin foil and stick it in the oven at about 250 degrees. Take the butter out of the fridge so it can soften a bit. At this point your olive oil will be bubbling slightly, your broccoli rabe will be tender, and your linguine will be well on its way to al dente. Give it a stir. Feel competent and proud. You are halfway finished and look how little skin it was off your teeth, you cooking-hater.

6. Create anticipation. When the linguine itself is almost done (usually it takes about ten minutes), lower the heat under the garlic pan a bit, and toss the broccoli rabe into the oil-and-garlic pan with an enormously satisfying explosion of sizzling sounds. Your guest will be driven mad with desire for you as you stir this whole thing together, releasing steam and the wonderful smell of garlic. The broccoli rabe will now soak up the flavors of the oil and the garlic, just as you will now soak up your guest's approbation and possibly secret, white-hot longing. This is your moment to set the salad and the bread and butter out on the table, and pour a little wine for yourself and your guest. Exchange some flirty glances. Promise everything will be ready in a minute. Leave them wanting more.

7. Combine everything. When the linguine is done, drain it, turn off the heat under the garlic–oil–broccoli rabe pan, and toss the linguine into the pan. Mix all the ingredients together.

8. Serve immediately, sprinkled with much good parmesan cheese. You are done. You look good. Your house smells amazing. You are a hero.

19.

How to Whistle with Your Fingers

Why You Should Learn This

The ear-popping taxi-stopping finger whistle has about a million practical applications in everyday life. There are certain uses, however, that all aspiring finger-whistlers should know are strenuously frowned upon:

Whistle	Don't Whistle
to hail a cab	to hail a waiter
to express admiration for a band or sports team	to express admiration for someone's butt

to alert someone to possible danger	to get someone's attention, unless they're about to be hit by a bus

How To

Bad news: The only way to learn this is to practice, practice, practice, and adjust the directions that follow depending on what seems to yield the best results for your particular mouth. I wish there was a foolproof mouth alignment for everybody. There's not. You're going to get spitty and out of breath and people will look at you funny. But it's worth it. Here are a couple of techniques to start trying.

Curled-Tongue Style

1. Stick your tongue out.

2. Curl your tongue inward (obviously this won't work for those of you who can't curl your tongue).

3. With the thumb and index finger of one hand, pinch the tongue by the sides about halfway back.

4. Fold the tongue back on itself at a steep angle with your thumb and index finger, so that your fingertips point in toward each other.

5. Close your lips around your fingers (which should be in your mouth, up to a bit past the first knuckle).

6. Tuck your lips tightly under your teeth.

7. Blow air (quick, hard bursts of air are best) down over the steep angle of your tongue.

Two-Handed Tongue-Tuck Style

1. Tuck your lips over your teeth tightly.

2. Fold the tip of your tongue over with your two index

fingers, such that the fingertips point to each other at about a ninety-degree angle (without touching), and your fingers are inside your mouth up to just past the first knuckle. If your tongue feels slippery and you can't keep it folded over with just your index fingers, reinforce with your middle fingers.

3. Angle your fingers and the tip of your tongue down toward the bottom of your mouth.

4. Blow down over the angle of your tongue.

Practice everywhere you feasibly can: at baseball games, at concerts, while walking down the street. Most people who see you will understand what you're up to, and you'd be surprised at how encouraging and supportive random strangers can be when they see someone attempting to acquire a new skill. Even when their fingers are covered with spit.

20.

How to Take Good Pictures

Why You Should Learn This

You should consider it a personal challenge when someone objects, "Oh, I never look good in pictures." Everyone who says this is secretly hoping that *you* will turn out to be the person she or he's been waiting for, the person who will, at last, given the right lighting and enough time, take the long-hoped-for picture in which she or he does not look like an Orc.

You may be familiar with the humility born of getting back a disappointing roll of film—twenty-seven shots that missed the mark, a packet of glossy double chins and red-eyed monsters and people with telephone poles growing out of their heads. But everybody looked so good in the little camera-hole-thing, you think morosely.

Most people are not taught the tricks that make good pictures; they're just sent out into the world with Polaroids to wreak havoc. Here are the rules that will make you a better picture taker—and, perhaps more importantly for the majority of us who don't sleep with *Smithsonian* or *National Geographic* under our pillows, a better photographer of people.

How To

Consider the Lighting

Photography manuals all start with one blithely misleading little rule: "Keep the light behind you to diminish sunglare." They're referring to glare on the camera lens, because presumably their lenses are all they think about. But when you're photographing people, following this rule to the letter means *face* glare: The light is full in someone's face on a sunny day, rendering that someone squinty, uncomfortable, and washed-out. If the light is strong, try keeping the sun over your left or right shoulder rather than at your back (and directly in your subject's eyes). More helpful lighting tips:

- Take pictures in the morning and early evening, and avoid taking them at high noon.

- Remember your flash is good for only about ten feet.

• The light won't look the same on film as it does to you in the moment you take the picture: A bright day will usually look brighter, and an overcast day or dim room will look dimmer.

Frame the Subject

Lighting aside, the most important thing to remember is that you are the master of your own destiny: Only *you* can control where things are in the picture. If that kind of power freaks you out, it may help to recall that every image has to be

Look for visual frames to give your pictures depth.

turned into a 4 × 6 two-dimensional rectangle, no more, no less. All you have to concentrate on is what goes into that rectangle, and what gets left out. Some tips that should help:

• Move in close. If you do nothing else, moving in close or zooming in will probably make your 4 × 6 two-dimensional rectangle more interesting: It eliminates visual clutter and provides a clear focal point. Try getting down to eye level for some close-ups, like a picture of a baby or an animal. Actually, this is fun for a number of reasons. Know what your dog's chin looks like? Find out.

• Try framing the subject deliberately off-center using the "rule of thirds." The rule of thirds is an age-old principle that basically speaks to the human eye's love of artful asymmetry; a rectangle with something or someone in the middle is not all that pleasing to the eye. To apply the rule of thirds, imagine two vertical lines dividing the picture into thirds left to right. Place your subject so that it falls on one of those lines—the remaining two-thirds should be background (or foreground). Now imagine two horizontal lines that divide the picture into thirds top to bottom, and make sure the horizon aligns with one of them. That's it. Rule of thirds. Boom. You can also try thinking of your picture as having a tic-tac-toe grid printed on it: Place your focus of interest on one of the points where the tic-tac-toe lines intersect, and align your horizon on one of the horizontal grid lines.

• Make sure you're not so focused on your subject that you don't notice problems with the background: poles, trees, signs, celestial objects, and animals that may appear to be coming out of someone's head.

Create Depth

While it's important to recall that every image will eventually be rendered two-dimensional in a picture, there are some easy ways to keep the picture from seeming flat and uninteresting, if you take your time and know what to look for.

"Leading lines" direct the viewer's eye to your subject.

- Try to incorporate lines—particularly diagonal lines—that will point a viewer's eyeballs to the subject of the picture. These can be railings, shadows, rivers, roads, train tracks, the planks of your porch—anything that helps literally "point" a viewer to what they should be looking at.

- Have a definite foreground and background.

- Look for frames. A frame can be any object at the periphery of an image that's closer to your camera than to your subject: a tree branch overhead, a door frame.

Help People Look Good

This is one of your most important responsibilities as a casual photographer. Fortunately, there are a surprising number of easy Photography 101 rules that actually help. If you remember even two of them you're bound to start taking better shots.

- Photograph your subjects from the waist up.

- Get in close—if the camera adds ten pounds, the best way to eliminate them is to not to show them at all. Besides, you want to remember their faces, not their shirts.

- Find a flattering angle. Eye level is good for most people; if you're photographing someone who's sensitive about having a heavy-looking face, taking the picture from slightly above usually helps.

• Reduce red-eye by having lots of light in the room (smaller pupils means less red-eye) or by telling your subjects to look about a foot over your head as you take the picture.

• When you're taking a group shot, don't try to get a full-body picture of everyone. Get close enough and aim high enough that the frame is filled with faces and heads, rather than arms and legs.

• Always use your flash—it helps diminish under-eye circles and flatten out skin irregularities.

• Be sneaky. Informal shots are almost always better than formal ones. Instead of asking people to pose and say "evil," catch them unawares as they're talking, thinking, moving, or laughing. You have to try really hard to take a *bad* picture of somebody laughing.

Backgrounds

Position your friends and relations in front of something attractive that won't look stark, and can absorb the light from the flash.

Good backgrounds

- grass (photograph someone sitting in the yard from above, so that the grass itself becomes the backdrop—this is clever both because the bright color makes a nice contrast and because double chins disappear from above)

- trees, flowers, bushes, anything verdant

- the horizon in the morning or evening

- doorways

Bad backgrounds

- white or black walls

- mirrors

- glossy wallpaper

- the horizon at high noon

- windows (unless they're open, the glass will usually reflect a glare)

Ugly backgrounds

- brick or cement walls

- parking lots, cars, or driveways

Be aware of problems with the background.

• all the other random strangers at the beach, or at graduation, or in the restaurant, or wherever you happen to be (get in close enough that your subjects are the only people in the frame)

Know When Not to Take a Picture

The following scenarios usually make for jumbled, difficult, and/or embarrassing pictures—so be aware of when to wait, and when to just put the camera away.

- Meals. Smeared lipstick and plates of half-eaten food don't make the best pictures.

- Crowded restaurants. You're going to annoy other diners, and probably inadvertently get some of them in your shot. Also, the risk of red-eye in restaurant photos is unusually high, since most restaurants are dim and you can't control the lighting.

- Parties at which people are bound to get drunk. A roll of film that begins at cocktail hour will usually come to no good.

- Concerts

- Landmarks after dusk

- Most street scenes. There's the random-unwanted-people issue, plus the likelihood of glare off of sidewalks, cars, and buildings.

- The beach. Does she want a picture of herself in a bathing suit? Are you sure? Are you really, really sure?

Skills Your Grandparents Had
That You Should Have Too

21.

How to Fold a Fitted Sheet

Why You Should Learn This

Many people can and do go through life blissfully unaware of how to fold a fitted sheet without making it a wadded-up lump. Once every three weeks or so, on laundry day, you may give it a halfhearted shot and surrender after a few minutes, thinking, Who's going to see this anyway? Who cares? The answer is: Nobody cares. *You* don't even care, admit it. In terms of making the world a better, safer place, it's utterly immaterial whether or not you can fold a fitted sheet neatly. By all means, learn the Heimlich, know how to change a flat tire, know how to jump a car—those are necessary skills without which you or somebody else may get into serious trouble. But the fact is, not all life skills are really a question of life or death. And that's precisely why this is such a cool thing to know how to do.

How To

If, once, in a moment of frustration at the laundromat, you burst out with, "How the hell are you supposed to fold these things anyway?," you may have gotten some enigmatic advice: "Fold the corners on top of each other." Incomprehensible as this sounds, that's actually exactly how it's done—but to this Grand Unified Theory of sheets, you must also add the knowledge of the right order in which to fold the corners on top of each other, as well as which way the seams should point. The following instructions work best with fitted sheets that have long or fairly loose elastic strips—if your sheets have very tight or small elastic strips, it's a little harder and your ultimate folded rectangle won't be as perfect. But it'll still look better than the usual wadded-up job.

1. You are standing in front of a clean, flat surface, where you've been successfully folding the rest of your laundry . . . till now. You have a fitted sheet. You are bewildered. Start by holding the sheet up by two adjacent elasticized corners, inside out.

2. Corner 1: Point an index finger into one fitted corner so that your hand is inside the corner of the sheet, and the edge of the (inside out) seam runs along your finger.

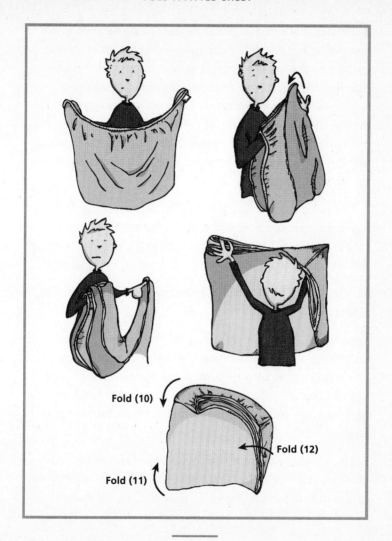

Fold (10)

Fold (11)

Fold (12)

3. Corner 2: There's a corner in your other hand (if you dropped it already, slide your hand along the elastic until you get to the nearest seam). Put your other index finger into this corner, so that the seam is inside out and runs along your finger. Now bring the tip of this finger up and over to meet the first, and let corner 2 fold over corner 1 on your finger. The seam of corner 2 should now be right-side out and hanging over your index finger, in alignment with the seam of corner 1.

4. Corner 3: Look down at the sheet. The corner that's hanging in front should be the one that's adjacent to corner 2. Pick it up and fold it over the other two, inside out, with all the seams aligned.

5. Corner 4: The last dangling corner gets folded over the others right-side out.

6. Now that you've corralled all the wily corners on one index finger, you should have two loops of elastic hanging down by your wrist (or elbow, if the elastic's super loose). Slip the thumb and index finger of your other hand into the bottom loop, and the third and fourth finger into the top loop.

7. Now, slide your hand away with your palm facing forward, so that you're holding a shape as shown at the bottom of the illustration on page 215. Give the sheet a shake to encourage all the folds to fall into place. Below the index finger with all the corners hanging from it, the sheet should fall in a more or less straight line. Below your other hand, it probably won't look so straight.

8. Lay both hands down flat on the folding surface in front of you, and slide your hands out of the sheet.

9. Smooth the sheet out so you have a rectangular shape that's a little rounded on the elasticized sides.

10. Fold the top over.

11. Fold the bottom over.

12. Fold the remaining elasticized side in.

You now should have a perfectly neat rectangle, the envy of all the other lost souls at the laundromat.

22.

How to Remove Common Stains

Why You Should Learn This

Of all the lost arts, stain fighting is probably the most regrettable body of knowledge to have fallen into the generation gap. It's sort of too bad younger generations like mine were never taught the lindy hop, but it's a crying shame that nobody born after 1970 knows a foolproof way to get out a grass stain.

How To

Know Your Stain-Fighting Technique

Most stains come out more easily with hard, fast blotting, as opposed to rubbing. "Blotting" usually connotes dabbing gently at something—imagine a sped-up, high-intensity version of that and you're on the right track. Getting out a stain takes a hard, fast, pounding motion. Blotting breaks up the stain and lifts it off the fibers of your clothes or tablecloth better than rubbing, and blotting also tends to distribute the stain-fighting formula or detergent better than rubbing. If you don't have anything to blot with, pinch two parts of the stained fabric between your fingers and blot (in other words, pound them together). If you absolutely can't resist the temptation to rub, rub only small sections at a time.

One of the best things to blot a stain with, if you use it correctly, is an old, clean toothbrush, because the bristles help break up stains quickly. You must resist the natural temptation to scrub back and forth with the toothbrush, though. Instead, hold the toothbrush close to the top, with your index finger behind the head, and use your index finger to make short, swift, forceful taps with the toothbrush bristles across the stain (pretreated with the appropriate stain-fighting solvent, as suggested below). When you're finished, rinse the toothbrush well and reuse it on your next stain.

Have the Right Tools on Hand

A bottle of prewash stain remover and a bottle of enzyme detergent are your best investments for everything regular old detergent can't vanquish—and that's a lot, unfortunately. For immediate, emergency removal of a fresh stain, you can blot or sponge with prepackaged wetnaps. Wetnaps, as I've advocated previously in these pages, are your best, dorkiest friends. Buy a package and suddenly you'll be amazed at how many things you'll want to attack with a moist towelette—and even more gratifying, how many things deserve, nay, demand to be attacked with a moist towelette.

Specific stain-fighting instructions for various common stains follow—some stains can be treated in a variety of ways, which are listed in no particular order (that is, it's hard to say which works best on blood: hydrogen peroxide or meat tenderizer). Pick whichever method seems most appropriate, or uses ingredients you actually have lying around.

Stain-Fighting Techniques for Specific Stains

Blood

• Make a paste of two parts cornstarch and one part cold water, allow it to dry on the stain (soaking up the blood), then brush it off. Wash in cold water.

• Cover the stain with nonseasoned meat tenderizer, then add cold water and let it soak for fifteen to thirty minutes. Wash in cold water.

• Wet the stain immediately with hydrogen peroxide (the antiseptic stuff) and let it bubble for five minutes, then rinse in cold water.

• Soak immediately in cold water, rub detergent or soap into the stain and blot vigorously, then wash in cold water.

Sweat

• Dissolve a quarter cup of salt in a pot of hot water, soak the stain in it for fifteen minutes. Then wash as usual.

Wine

• Pour table salt over the stain immediately, which will absorb some of the wine. Then soak the fabric in cold water.

• Rinse thoroughly and immediately with cold water.

• Soak the stain for twenty minutes in a mixture of equal parts cool water and detergent, with a splash of white vinegar. Then wash in warm water.

Oil and Grease

• Squirt on some shampoo for oily hair and let it soak for an hour, then wash in hot water.

• Sprinkle talcum powder or cornstarch on the spot while it's still wet; let the powder dry and brush it off.

Lipstick and Makeup

• Allow some non–oil-based makeup remover to sink in, then blot the stain out.

Ink

• Saturate with alcohol-based non-oil hairspray, then wash.

• Saturate with isopropyl alcohol, then blot with a paper towel and rub in regular detergent. Wash as usual.

Mud

• Let the mud dry first! Then beat as much of the dried mud off as you can, and rub in some laundry detergent. Wash as usual.

Grass

• Soak in an enzyme presoak for twenty minutes, then wash as usual.

• If the fabric is colorfast (meaning it won't bleed), moisten the stain with a sponge dipped in isopropyl alcohol. Let the alcohol soak in, then wash.

Ketchup and Tomato Sauce

- Blot hard with a baby wipe or towelette.

- Soak in an enzyme presoak for fifteen minutes, then wash.

Food (including chocolate and dark juices)

- Either of the remedies listed for ketchup and tomato sauce should work.

- If you spill something on yourself at a restaurant, sneak off to the bathroom and soak the stain in a good dollop of spit—the ingredients in spit that break down food in your mouth also help break it down outside your mouth. Then blot hard with a warm, wet paper towel.

23.

How to Sew on a Button

Why You Should Learn This

If you've ever experienced a true button-popping emergency, you know exactly why it's so important to be able to repair the damage efficiently and swiftly. That said, of course, not every lost button is an emergency. Not all buttons pop off—some linger on loose threads, some fall off mysteriously in the closet. These are the kinds of buttons we convince ourselves nobody will notice are missing. There's a fine line between disheveled and sloppy, and it's pretty easy to tell when somebody *else* has crossed it. Missing buttons, stains, yellow teeth, down-at-heel shoes—less-than-perfect grooming is glaringly obvious on other people, and mysteriously difficult to see on ourselves. Your favorite grotty sweater with the missing button doesn't make *you* look like a bag lady, no no. The interviewer won't notice the missing button on *your* blazer, especially not if you leave it open (you're so clever).

You should learn to sew on a button because your mind is playing tricks on you: While you may believe nobody will notice, somebody probably will. And they'll wonder why you left the house in such a state of disrepair.

How To

1. Gather your tools. You'll need:

- Your button

- Thread that matches the thread in the other buttons

- A pencil or thin piece of chalk

- Someplace comfy to sit with good, strong light

- Scissors

- A sewing needle that has a decent-sized eye, and that can pierce the fabric easily—sewing a button on a cotton shirt takes a regular old needle; sewing a button on a winter coat requires a needle that's considerably thicker and a bit longer. Most cheap sewing kits include delicate needles with teeny tiny holes. You can buy a good package of easier-to-use needles at most big drugstores, or at any fabric store.

2. Figure out where to place the button. If the button fell off recently, you may be able to see the old holes where the thread used to be, and resew the button into the exact same spot. If the old holes are no longer visible, then you need to figure out where the button should go. Button up the shirt (or pants or what have you), and pull the placket (or waistband or what have you) as taut and straight as you can. Put your pencil through the center of the buttonhole that's missing its button and make a light mark—don't worry, it'll wash off. If the fabric is black, dip your pencil lead in baking soda and then make a light mark, or use a piece of chalk. This mark is where you should center your button.

3. Cut the thread. For most jobs, about a foot and a half should do. Sewing a button back on a coat may require more like two feet. Use scissors, not your teeth—a gnawed-off thread is much harder to get through a needle.

4. Thread the needle. There are numerous ways to do this.

• Use a threader. A threader is one of those little foil disk things with a loop of wire at the end. Grasp the threader by the foil disk, and stick the loop of wire all the way through the eye of your needle. Now stick the end of your thread into the wire loop and pull about three or four inches through. Then you can pull the wire loop back out, which brings your thread along with it, right through the eye of the needle.

● Use spit: the universal solvent *and* problem solver. Give the end of your thread a good wetting, and position the needle so that it's between your light source and you. Pinch the thread between your thumb and forefinger so that there's about a half inch of wet thread sticking out, then aim that end straight into the eye of the needle, and pull the thread through. (It's really not so hard if you have a needle with a hole that's actually detectable by the human eye; so again, consider chucking the ones in that sewing kit you stole from the Marriott.)

● Use a crease. Hold the needle horizontally, so you can't see the eye. Drape the thread over the needle and pull hard, making a crease in the thread. Pinch the crease to reinforce it. Then hold the needle's eye between you and the light source, and guide the crease through the eye of the needle (a little spit doesn't hurt here either) until you can pinch it on the other side and pull it through.

5. Pull the thread halfway through and make a knot with the two ends. Don't worry about making the knot close to the ends of the threads, just snip off any long trailing bits afterward.

6. Center the button on the mark you made (unbutton the garment first), or align the old needle holes with the button holes. Hold the button in place with one hand.

7. Now you're almost ready to start sewing. Are you sitting under a good strong light? Great. Nice and comfy? Excellent. Have you taken the time to check out how the other buttons are sewn on? Hmm. Now's the time to do that if you haven't already. You want your button-repair job to be as indistinguishable from all the other buttons as possible.

Two-hole buttons or metal-loop buttons are fairly obvious, they can be stitched on only one way. Four-hole buttons can be stitched on in a few different ways: with the thread making an X, with the thread making two parallel lines, and with the thread making a square.

8. Start your first stitch underneath the fabric, at the top buttonhole, or at the top left button hole if it's a four-hole button. Guide your needle up through the fabric, then up through the buttonhole. Pull all the way to the knot at the end of the thread.

9. Sew on the button. Once you've made that first stitch, the rest is pretty much a piece of cake. Here's how to continue stitching the most common types of buttons:

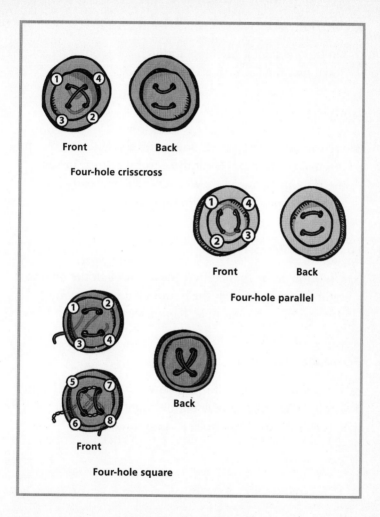

Front   Back

Four-hole crisscross

Front   Back

Four-hole parallel

Front

Back

Four-hole square

Metal loop

Up on one side of the loop, through the loop, and back down into the fabric. Repeat five times.

Two-hole

Up through the top hole, down into the bottom hole and through the fabric. Repeat three to four times, or until the amount of thread showing over the button holes is about the same as all the other buttons.

Four-hole crisscross

Up through the top left hole, down through the bottom right hole. Up through the bottom left hole, down through the top right hole. Repeat three times.

Four-hole parallel

Up through the top left hole, down through the bottom left hole. Up through the bottom right hole, down through the top right hole. Repeat three times.

Four-hole square

Up through the top left hole, down through the top right hole. Up through the bottom left hole, down through the bottom right hole. Up through the top left hole, down through the bottom left hole. Up through the top right hole, down through the bottom right hole. Repeat twice.

10. Cut the needle off the thread inside the fabric, under the button.

11. Tie a knot with the loose ends and snip off any long trailing bits.

Troubleshooting

I'm sewing a button back on a coat, and all the other buttons have this little ball of thread underneath them. What is that? Can I do that? Yes, you can and should. The little ball of thread is probably about as thick as the fabric—it's what makes the buttons buttonable. Before you make a stitch, slide a toothpick, matchstick, or one of those little stirrer straws between the fabric and the button. Sew the button on, then after your last stitch, with the needle under the fabric, slide the toothpick out while holding the button in place. Bring the needle up through the fabric again, wrap the thread tightly around the connecting threads a few times, then poke the needle back through the fabric under the button and tie a knot.

The best skills are the simplest.

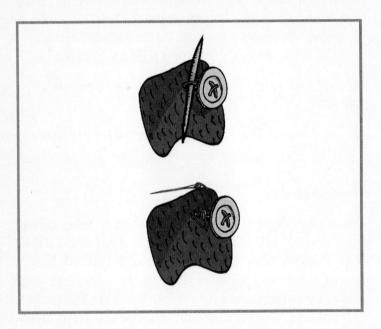

24.

How to Carve Turkey, Lasagna, and Birthday Cake

Why You Should Learn This

Imagine this: You are, say, forty. A child of yours is having a birthday party. As you hand each child at the party a twisted, ragged, twelve-car-pile-up piece of birthday cake on a festive paper plate smeared with globs of renegade frosting, one of the other mothers chirps brightly, "I can take over from here. You just rest."

Or this: You are older. Your parents and grandparents are older still. It's Thanksgiving. The all-day cooking and hefting of an enormous yard-bird has wiped your mom and grandma out. Dad and grandpa are sleeping the sleep of the dead in front of the game, and it's clear that the carving of the bird has to fall to somebody else this year. Your smartypants younger sibling, the one your parents really love, chirps brightly, "No problem, Mom, I know how to carve poultry!"

Or this: You are in Italy. You are conducting an important transaction with the Mafia. Negotiations have been tense, and the big man has invited you to his mother's house for dinner to finish the discussion. As the honored guest, you are asked to cut and serve the lasagna. If you fail, you will almost certainly be shot.

It's good not to fail.

How To Carve a Turkey

Before You Start

• Let the bird rest for twenty minutes after removing it from the oven. It has to settle and collect itself, and you'll be really, really sorry (and greasy, and messy, and known forever after as "the one who turned a beautiful turkey into thousands of little flecks of meat") if you don't let that happen.

• Use this time to find the very sharpest knife in the kitchen, and two long serving forks.

• Also find a big cutting board. In fact, you may want to find two: one for cutting the body of the bird and one for carving the legs when you remove them.

- Have a platter ready for the slices.

- Put on an apron and/or tuck in your tie.

- Wash your hands.

The Messy Part

A turkey's dark meat comes primarily from the leg and thigh, and that's what you want to carve first—dark meat doesn't dry out as quickly as white meat, so it can withstand a wait on the serving platter while you do the rest of the slicing. But be warned: This part of the operation is the messiest and most physical, so you may want to do it in the kitchen out of sight, rather than at the table. When you're wrasslin' yard-bird it usually loses, but it's still not pretty. Just take the carving of the bird one step at a time, and you'll be fine.

1. Move the bird from the roasting pan to the carving board. This can be tricky with large, heavy, stuffed turkeys, especially since most people don't own a big roasting pan and rack, and tend to make their Thanksgiving turkeys in those wobbly, disposable aluminum pans from the grocery store. In fact, getting one of those aluminum pans out of the oven without a major incident is an accomplishment in itself— you're basically balancing a ten-pound-plus bird and a sloshy reservoir of grease and juices on a big piece of tinfoil.

• Put the cutting board right next to the oven pan roasting on the counter.

• Carefully wedge one long serving fork into the chest cavity of the bird, and poke another serving fork into the neck. Let the tines of the fork go solidly into the meat—really dig it in there or you won't have enough leverage. When you think you have a good, evenly balanced handle on the turkey, quickly heft the bird out of the pan with the forks and drop it onto the cutting board. There will probably be a mess. It's okay. Messes can be cleaned.

• Orient the cutting board so that you're comfortable—for some people this will mean looking straight down at the breast, for some it will mean having the bird's neck to your left (if you're right-handed) or right (if you're left-handed). For the directions that follow, your writing hand is your knife hand, and your fork hand is whichever hand you're not cutting with.

• Cut whatever was used to truss the legs.

2. Remove the legs.

• Pull the drumstick away from the body with your fingers, and with your other hand, use your knife to cut the skin between the leg and the body. You should find that this loosens the leg somewhat.

CARVE TURKEY, LASAGNA, AND CAKE

- Now use the flat end of your knife on the inside of the leg to press the leg even farther away from the body, at an angle to the cutting board.

- Use your carving fork to hold the leg in position.

- Find the thigh joint (as opposed to the drumstick joint, the one that's easy to see) by poking delicately into the crevice with your knife point. Sometimes this joint can be surprisingly hard to locate: Start at the very top of the crease between leg and body and angle the knife in, and you're almost sure to hit it. If you hit something hard (the backbone) you've angled in too far.

- Cut through the ligaments to separate the joint.

- Now that the leg is off, you want to separate the drumstick from the thigh. Spear the thigh to the cutting board with your carving fork, and cut through the ligaments of the drumstick joint.

- Repeat all the steps on the other side—you may find it gives you more leverage to reorient the cutting board. Since I've already used the word *leverage* twice, it should be clear to you by now that leverage is everything.

3. Carve the drumsticks. It's hard to get slices of meat off a drumstick neatly, so don't sweat the aesthetics and consider this your warmup round—finding your knife grip, getting your technique solid, discovering your carving mojo, and all that.

- Using your fork hand, hold the drumstick upright by the bone end, so that the meaty part is on the cutting board.

- Place your knife edge about two thirds of the way down the drumstick and slice downward at a slight angle to the bone.

- Turn the drumstick and repeat, starting your slices from higher and higher up on the leg until you've got most of the meat off.

- Use your fingers to pick off any extra bits. Go ahead. It's family. They'll never know.

4. Carve the thighs. Ah, delicious, delicious thigh. Truly the tastiest part of the turkey. They are easier to cut than the drumsticks, but take your time and make straight, long slices, or you'll have the rabid dark-meat fans scowling at you all through dinner.

- Lay the thigh flat on the cutting board, bony side down.

- Figure out where the bone is by finding the joints on both ends; the bone runs straight through.

- There will usually be less meat on one side of the bone than on the other. Start at the point farthest from the bone on the meatier side of the thigh, and cut the meat at a downward angle, in lines parallel to the bone. Use your carving fork to hold each thigh slice in place as you go . . . again, it's about leverage.

- To carve the less meaty side, hold the thigh upright at the joint just like you did the drumsticks. Then cut the meat off at a downward angle—also just like you did with the drumsticks.

- Repeat with the other thigh. By this point the act of carving downward on an upright-angled bone should be getting easier for you. Which is good, because next year you won't make such a mess out of the drumsticks.

- Again, furtively pick any remaining bits of meat off with your fingers.

At this point, most of the messy work is done. Someone should decide whether the breast will be carved at the table, and whether to remove the stuffing now or as the white meat is being carved. These traditions vary from family to family; everybody has their own little way of doing things. But if the decision is made to do stuffing-retrieval and breast-carving at the table, you'll have one more thing to accomplish in the secret lair of the kitchen:

5. Make a hole to remove stuffing. This step makes the re-trieval of the stuffing a little less visually jarring: Spooning it out of the, er, hole you stuffed it into is fine, but it may be preferable to make a side exit.

- Look at the holes where the legs used to be and decide which one is bigger and jaggedier.

- There should be some softer tissue around the hole; use your knife to cut a wider opening.

- Spoon stuffing out from this opening at the table.

The Less-Messy Part

Following a brief cleanup session for you and your utensils, bring the turkey to the table (or don't, if that's the way it's done in your house). Since you want to leave white meat on the bone as long as possible so it doesn't dry out, you'll probably only want to carve one side of the breast to start, and then go back to carve more when people want seconds.

1. Make a cut deep into the breast, parallel to the wing.

- Nestle your knife edge into the crevice between the wing and the body.

- From there, make a long deep cut straight across, in toward the center of the bird.

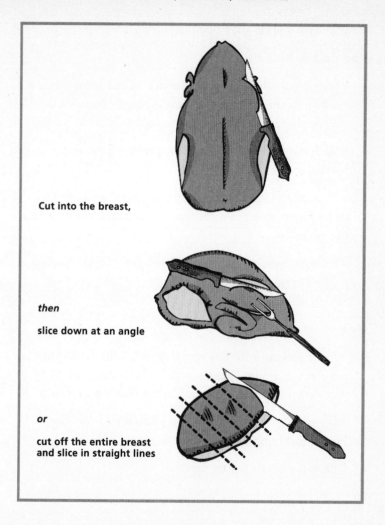

Cut into the breast,

then

slice down at an angle

or

cut off the entire breast
and slice in straight lines

2. Carve the breast.

The on-the-bird way

- Starting about halfway up the side of the breast, slice thinly into the meat at a downward angle. Imagine the rib cage and angle your knife parallel to it.

- Slice the meat all the way down to that first, wing–parallel cut.

- The meat should fall away as you get down to this line, so be sure to spear it with your carving fork before it hits the table.

- Continue slicing, following the curve of the breast up to the breastbone.

The off-the-bird way

- After making your cut across in step 1, make another, perpendicular cut from the top of the breastbone all the way down into the breast until your two cuts intersect.

- Remove the entire breast and place it on a cutting board or serving platter, skin side up.

- Slice the breast left to right.

Troubleshooting

I'm trying to cut slices of meat but it's falling apart all over the place. You didn't let the bird sit quite long enough before you started cutting: It needs fifteen minutes to a half hour to get firm and collected. Just wait a little longer. Don't worry, it won't get cold.

Uncle Bob wants the neck. What the hell is that? Can you actually eat it? The neck is usually tucked under the bird when you first get it from the shop—if you are just now discovering that you didn't remove the neck and giblets before roasting the turkey, it's time to start calling Chinese restaurants for takeout. If you removed the neck and giblets before roasting (and you must), you can simmer the neck in a saucepan with 6 cups of water and some of the juices from the roasting pan for a couple of hours while the turkey finishes, and then pull off the neck meat and discard the bony parts. The neck is sort of like juicy, stringy dark meat. Some people dig that.

The kids want to do the wishbone thing. Where do I find it? It's a good idea to remove the wishbone to make the breast easier to carve, and it's probably easiest to do so when you're stuffing the turkey, but you can remove it after the bird cooks as well. Poke delicately around the top of the neck hole until you feel something hard; that's most likely the wishbone. Use your knife to cut around the bone until it's exposed, and then just pull it out. Boil it in water for about ten minutes to remove the oil and meat, and let it dry out.

What's the best way to store all the leftover meat? Within two hours of taking the turkey from the oven, remove all the stuffing and put it in a plastic container in the fridge. Wrap all the dark meat in tinfoil. White meat you want to leave uncarved as long as possible. Cut the meat off the breast in as whole a chunk as you can and wrap it in tinfoil to store; cut off only as much as you're going to use at once when you're eating leftovers.

How to Cut Lasagna

This is much like cutting a rectangular in-pan cake (see How to Cut a Cake), except cake doesn't trail long bits of melty cheese (don't we all wish it did!—but that's probably why lasagna was invented). The melty cheese and globby noodles, however, can make it nearly impossible to serve an intact piece of fresh lasagna. So the question is, how do you avoid presenting your lasagna as a mound of steaming red and yellow stuff?

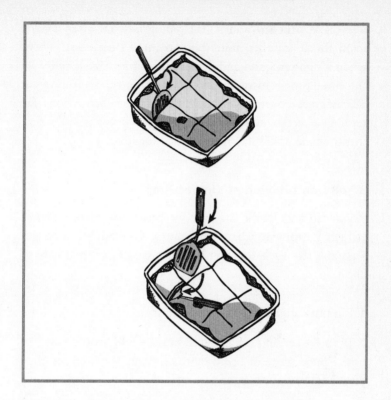

The Secret Sneaky Trick to Serving Intact Pieces of Lasagna

As anybody who has eaten leftover lasagna knows, it actually tastes better after it's been reheated. Why? The noodles are firmer and the sauces and cheeses are more integrated. So after you've baked it and it's all piping hot, let your lasagna stand for at least an hour (but no more than two). Then, when it's gotten good and firm again, cut it twice lengthwise and three times crosswise, and reheat it for fifteen minutes at 325 degrees covered with foil. Follow the instructions for serving a rectangular in-pan cake below—you should find that the pieces will stay mostly stuck together.

If You Don't Have that Kind of Time . . .

If you can only let the lasagna collect itself for fifteen minutes (which is really the bare minimum), you can still cut and serve mostly-stuck-together lasagna pieces. But you'll have to cheat.

1. Find two equal-sized, slatted spatulas.

2. If you're serving lasagna with bread—why would you not?—put a piece of bread on the serving plate and put the plate next to your lasagna pan.

3. Make two lengthwise and three crosswise cuts in the lasagna with a sharp knife. Wipe melted cheese off the blade as often as necessary.

4. Starting at a corner, insert one spatula into the lasagna along the crosswise cut, and slide it under the slice.

5. Stick the second spatula vertically into the lasagna along the lengthwise cut.

6. Hold the vertical spatula in place as you carefully lift the piece out with the first spatula.

7. Swiftly transfer the slice to the serving plate, sliding it onto the plate so that the long side is resting against the piece of bread (this is the retaining wall that will help keep the lasagna piece from spilling its delicious inner layers all over the plate).

8. For all successive slices, slide the first spatula under the piece, and use the second spatula to reinforce the cuts you made. Then leave the second spatula stuck in one of the cuts to shore up the lasagna while you lift out the piece, and quickly slide the lasagna slice onto a plate right snug up against a piece of bread.

How to Cut a Cake

Be warned: At weddings, catering people are paid a dollar or so per slice to do what you are about to attempt. So if you get snarked by some other mom at the birthday party, shrug it off and keep going.

Before You Start

• Make sure you have the right knife. The right knife is long (8 inches or so), thin, and serrated. It is not a butter knife. It is not a steak knife. It is a little like a bread knife, if that's all you've got lying around.

• Get a cake server or spatula (preferably smallish and/or triangular).

• Have a hot wet towel at hand to wipe all the icing buildup off the blade.

• If you can, find a partner in crime who can provide a steady supply of cake plates for you to tip slices onto. Two people can cut a cake faster than one, and at a kids' birthday party—or indeed, any situation involving hungry people and cake—time is of the essence.

• Cake is like turkey in one (and only one) sense: It will dry out if you expose it to the air. So cut as much as you're going to eat and leave the rest intact.

Note that the directions that follow allow for neat, good-sized cake slices, but they eschew professional caterers' recommended slice sizes for economical cake-cutting, because those are just too damn small. Rather, these directions are intended to ensure that everybody will feel like they got a nice, solid chunk of cake (in other words a couple of inches bigger than a caterer would have cut).

If Your Cake Is Rectangular . . .

1. With the long, serrated knife (*not* the short, triangular cake server): Cut one long line down the cake lengthwise,

about 3 inches from the side of the cake, if the cake was baked in a standard 9-×-13-inch pan, or 2 inches if it's a smaller rectangle.

2. Make a horizontal cut across, about 2 inches from the end of the cake.

3. Now it's time for the cake server—this part of the operation is best done with two hands. With one hand, slide your cake server under the slice carefully. With the other hand, slide your knife into the far side of the incision.

4. Use the cake server and knife in tandem to tip the slice onto a cake plate, provided, if you are lucky, by your cake-cutting partner. Hand the plate to an eager bystander or your cake-cutting partner, who can distribute it appropriately while you cut the next slice. It's better to tip the slices, rather than attempting to lift them whole out of the cake. Tipping increases the likelihood that the cake slice won't get all mangled. Of course, this assumes that your rectangular cake was actually removed from the cake pan before it was frosted and served, which is not always the case. If your cake is still in utero, that is, in the pan, you must, alas, start with a sort of sac-bunt cake slice, like so:

- Find a regular old wide spatula.

- Cut your first cake slice twice as wide as usual (4 inches), or as wide as the spatula you found.

• Slide your cake server vertically into the cake so it provides a sort of buttressing, leveraging wall against the uncut portion.

• Carefully slide your spatula into the cake pan and under the cake slice.

• Lift the cake slice out as cleanly as possible between the spatula and the cake server. The slice will probably get a little mushed on one side or other. The universe is imperfect.

• Put the double-wide, slightly mushed cake slice on a plate, cut it in half, move one half to another plate and serve.

5. Repeat cutting and tipping slices until you get to the end of the row. Wipe the icing off the blade with your towel as you go; the more icing buildup there is, the sloppier the slicing will get.

6. If people clamor for more cake, then cut another long line down the cake lengthwise, 3 inches from the edge.

7. Cut 2-inch slices down the row as before. Repeat until your greedy guests finally start exercising a little restraint.

If Your Cake Is Round . . .

1. Use your long thin knife to cut an inner circle, about 2 inches from the outer edge of the cake. If you have a really big round cake, move in another 2 inches and cut a second inner circle.

2. Make one cut from the outer edge of the outermost circle to the edge of the inner circle.

3. Make another cut two inches from the first.

4. Slide your cake server under the cake slice.

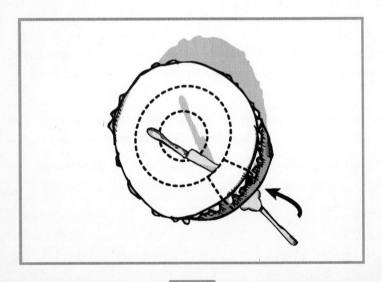

5. Slide your knife vertically into the cake at the tip of the slice, where the inner circle starts.

6. Use your knife to help scooch the cake slice out on the cake server. Slide the slice onto a plate.

7. Make a cut two inches away for your next slice.

8. Hold the cake server next to the slice so that the flat end is parallel to the cake.

9. Using your knife, carefully tip the slice onto the cake server, and use the flat side of the knife to hold the cake on the server as you slide the slice out and onto a plate.

10. For each successive slice around the outer circle, you should have enough room to cut a two-inch slice and simply tip it onto a plate with the cake server. Remember to wipe globs of icing off your knife as you go.

11. Before slicing the inner circle, cut a tiny, third circle at the core of the cake, about an inch in diameter.

12. Now cut the second circle the same way you did the first. Some lucky person gets a nifty little round piece of cake at the end.

25.

How to Hold a Baby

Why You Should Learn This

By the time you're thirty, some of your friends are going to start having babies, if they haven't already. Babies are soft and funny-looking and kind of excellent. They're little people, real actual people, with mysterious personalities inside them waiting to unfurl and develop. Imagine what they're going to be like when they grow up! Wow. Wouldn't it be great if you could be trusted to hold one with your big-clumsy-oaf paws?

Maybe you disagree, and you don't think babies are the least bit excellent. Maybe you weren't the baby-sitting type in high school. Maybe you don't even like kids that much—and you certainly don't plan on having one yourself anytime soon if you can help it. That's fine. But sooner or later, somebody you know and love is going to have a baby, and one day while you're over at his or her house, watching the inevitable baby-worship with barely concealed contempt, your friend will get tired or need to do something and ask somebody—maybe you—to hold the child, and when she or he does, know this: It's going to be hard to say "No, I'd rather not hold the baby. It's weird and smush-faced and it might start screaming."

Holding a baby—especially somebody else's baby—and making a mistake is one of those things you don't ever want to do, like "testing" a steel trap in the woods or looking for a good time in Saskatchewan. And even if you don't actually seek out babies to hold, chances are good that unless you have hooks for hands you will someday be asked to do it.

How To

Know the Basic Baby Rules

Always support the head. If you've never heard that rule before you probably shouldn't even look at a baby, much less hold one. Until they're six months old, babies don't have much control of their head and neck, and in fact for the first four to six weeks, a baby's head is actually heavier than its neck can handle, which is, frankly, a little creepy. Better safe than sorry: Unless the baby is six or seven months old, and/or you know it's definitely in control of its head and neck, hold the back of the baby's head with one hand, or support the head in the crook of your arm. Of course, babies' heads don't just snap off, but you should still be careful—they're not Weebles.

Move slowly and with confidence. Don't hesitate, fumble, swoop, or jerk the kid around. Just act like you do this every day. Babies can smell fear.

Keep the baby's body in a relatively compact bundle. Most babies prefer not to be splayed out all over your lap, unless you're talking about an "older baby," which sounds like an oxymoron but really just means a child closer to two years old. Kids approaching toddlerdom are just discovering all the different ways their bodies can move, and they plan to continue their explorations in your lap, whether or not that's especially comfortable for you.

Understand that the baby is really in charge. Once somebody hands you their baby you have no free will. You are furniture. You have no bladder to empty, no thirst to slake, no itch to scratch, no hunger to sate until somebody takes the baby off your hands. If you doubt this rule, just try testing it. See how much you like being to blame for the baby's hour-long crying jag.

The point is, while you're holding a baby, you should try to subsume your needs to hers. It's impossible for most of us to remember what it's like to be a baby, but when you think about it, for a baby the world must be simultaneously exciting and aggravating: Everybody's constantly picking you up and taking you places, shoving weird stuff in your mouth that you don't always like, you can hardly see anything, you can hardly sit up, everything exhausts you—being a baby must be sort of like having the flu. When you're holding a baby, try to be mindful that for her, sudden changes are uncool, shifting around is uncool, passing her off just to reach for the crudités is uncool. She's been through a lot, poor little scrapper. So sit still for God's sake.

Take Possession of the Baby without Dropping It

Before you get to hold the baby, somebody either has to hand her to you or you have to pick her up. There are several ways of doing this.

If the baby is a brand-new person, less than four months old, the best way for someone to hand her to you is *cradle style*:

• The hander-offer approaches you with the baby held cradle style: one hand under the back and bottom, with the baby's head supported by the crook of the arm. The other hand can be under the baby providing extra rump support, or touching the baby on the arm, tummy, or chest—which tends to be a comfort when all the shifting and switching starts.

- With the hander-offer standing quite close to you, slide the hand of your non-cradling arm (opposite the hander-offer's non-cradling arm) under the baby's head, in the crook of the hander-offer's arm.

- Bend your other elbow, holding your arm close to your body.

- The hander-offer now slides the baby's bottom and back into the crevice between your bent arm and your body, as you support the baby's head and gently ease it into the crook of your arm.

There's also *base-support style,* which is useful whether you're picking a baby up or having one passed to you. One side note: Remember, babies don't see very far, so before you pick a baby up, it's nice to alert them to the fact that you're there by rubbing their tummy or back for a few seconds. Surprising a baby with a trip through midair won't end well for either of you.

- Slide one of your hands under the baby's bottom and back (the "base").

- Put your other hand under the baby's neck and head.

- Lift or move the child from the base, with your arm bent close to your body, and your other hand supporting the

Base-support Style

Limp-bacon Style

baby's head. This takes a bit of upper-arm strength, but it's very comfortable for the baby to be moved around in this way. You can make eye contact the whole time, and/or possibly make a goony face, both of which babies tend to dig.

Finally, there's what you could call *limp-bacon style*: This is usually how a confident mom will pass an older baby to someone for a temporary lap visit. It's a little disconcerting for the kid, but to be honest, it's the easiest picking-up-and-passing method for mom (in terms of both wiggle restraint and her own arm muscles), which is why it's so popular.

• The hander-offer (or mom) approaches you with the child held by the rib cage under the armpits. In this way, the baby's arms are pretty much immobilized, the shoulders are shrugged up, providing some support for the head, and the legs are dangling like, well, limp bacon. From here, you have three options:

a) Take the child base-support style. Slide one hand under the baby's bottom, put the other behind its head, and take it into your lap;

b) Take the child by putting your hands around its rib cage, underneath the hander-offer's hands; the hander-offer then lets go and helps support the baby's head, if necessary, until you get the baby situated (see "Get the Baby Situated Without Making It Cry" below);

c) Let the hander-offer sit the child down right in your lap. Your only responsibilities in this case are to use one hand to move the baby's legs aside or out, so it can sit, and put your other hand behind the baby's neck and upper body for support.

Get the Baby Situated without Making It Cry

Once you do have the baby in hand, you are now compelled to either hold it in your lap, or carry it if you're standing. It's important not to jostle or shift the baby around too much once the baby lands on you, because it'll probably start crying. Find a comfortable position and hold it. The best thing to do is just ask the mom or dad how the baby likes to be held. Most moms and dads know, if only on a gut level, but they still may not pass along the information—maybe they don't know how to explain it, maybe they're too damn tired to explain it, maybe they don't want their baby to cotton to you too much anyway. In any case, if no helpful hints are forthcoming, holding a baby in your lap is deceptively easy and mostly comfortable:

• If it's a newborn who was passed to you cradle style, sit with the child cradle style in your arms, with your other arm either under the baby's bottom for support, or stroking/

tickling/rubbing the baby's tummy/nose/fingers. If the baby's asleep, of course, do none of these things. Just sit quietly and pray.

• If the baby's awake and not a newborn, you can situate the baby on your lap sitting up, either facing the room with its head and body resting against your belly and chest, or facing you, with your hands supporting the baby's upper back and neck. Be aware that if it's facing you, that means you'll have to entertain the baby.

Carrying a Baby

Carrying a baby is similarly easy, although less comfy, and there are a couple of ways to do it:

• Cradle style is still the best way to carry a newborn baby, whether you're sitting or standing.

• *Shoulder style:* Curve one forearm under the baby's bottom to support it. Rest the baby's head against your shoulder with the palm of your other hand on its neck and upper back, fingers supporting the head gently. If the baby is in control of its head and neck and doesn't need support, you can hoist the child up a little higher so that both your arms are supporting the baby's bottom, and the baby can watch over your shoulder as the world goes by in reverse. Plus, if the baby horks, most of it will miss your shirt.

Shoulder Style

Front-facing Style

Hip-carry Style

• *Front-facing style:* This is a fun way to carry a baby—especially one who's alert and interested in checking stuff out. Put one forearm under the baby's bottom and wrap the other around the baby's chest to hold her close to your rib cage so it feels safe. Now you can walk around and check stuff out together, which can be enormously satisfying for both of you. Just don't let the baby check out anything pointy.

• *Hip carry:* The crook of one arm under the baby's bottom, with the baby's legs on either side of your torso. Needless to say, this is only appropriate for older babies with head and neck control. The hip carry leaves you with a free arm, but it can be rather uncomfortable.

Troubleshooting

Do I have to wash my hands first? If the baby is a newborn, yes, you probably should—the immune system of a newborn isn't really up to snuff, and if you think a diaper is gross, you should see the germs and bacteria you have on your hands right now. If the baby is older, ask the parents what they prefer—they may prefer you to get your damn hands out of the sink and just hold the kid.

How do I give it back? Whether you're putting a baby down in its crib or handing it to someone else, keep the baby's body close to you for as long as possible. They don't like being thrust out into midair to be picked up by another pair of hands; rather, let the next person who wants to hold the baby come to you and take her in one of the ways described above. As the hander-offer, you will always release the baby's body in this order: butt first, head last. You should support the head until you're sure the other person has got it.

It's awake. I'm holding it. It's looking at me expectantly. What do I do? For your baby-entertaining edification:

Babies like	Babies do not like
repetition	sudden movements
funny noises	yelling
funny faces	being poked
"hiding" games where *you* hide	"hiding" games where *they* hide (they usually don't get it)
rocking or gentle bouncing	vigorous bouncing (some babies are weird, though)
curling their fingers around yours	having *their* fingers held

being close to you	floating (the "airplane" game is a lot more fun when you're old enough to *ask* for it)
things that you pretend amaze you	things that are clearly lame
songs you make up	most songs you know

26.

How to Change a Diaper

Why You Should Learn This

Most of the time, we try to get away with doing as little as possible for other people. Contrary to what older generations will try to tell you for the rest of your life, this avoidance trait is not new or unique to today's younger people. There's a reason why grousing about "kids these days" was always a popular pastime for old farts even when our grandparents were young. You are not to blame for the fact that our culture tolerates people who do as little as possible—and, in fact, rewards them richly, giving them media empires, television shows, magazine covers, and roles in big expensive movies. But there are times when doing as little as possible is wrong, truly morally insanely wrong, and one of those times is when a relative or a good friend of yours has a baby.

It will happen, make no mistake. And when it happens, and your loved one or good buddy becomes a sleep-deprived, glittery-eyed, blank-faced shell of awkwardly combined misery, joy, and helplessness, *you have got to put out.* You have to send flowers and presents. You have to squeal with delight. (Yes, men, even you: Start practicing now.) You have to volunteer to baby-sit. You have to go for a visit and be as helpful as possible while you're there, boiling bottles, holding the baby so the parents can have a break, entertaining the child in the high chair so the parents can get the mushy evil-smelling baby food ready. And no matter how you feel about it, no matter how gag prone or weak stomached or squeamish or lazy you are, you have to change a diaper or two.

How To

1. Know your assignment. Are you changing a cloth or a disposable diaper? Is it number one or number two? Is the baby a boy or a girl? Believe it or not, the answer to each of these questions makes a difference in what you're about to attempt.

2. Wash your hands.

3. Gather your weapons. You'll need:

- A clean diaper

- A clean towel or cloth

- Baby wipes

- A trash can with a lid, and a diaper pail if you're changing a cloth diaper

- Diaper pins or fasteners, if you're changing a cloth diaper

- Some parents also use baby powder or cornstarch to help avoid diaper rash and irritation. Ask.

4. Unfasten the baby's pants. This may seem obvious, but baby clothing is designed with cunning little snaps between the legs to facilitate this very operation. Just look for the snaps in the seat of the pants, and pull all the relevant clothing up and and well out of the way. You don't usually have to remove all of the baby's clothes to change a diaper—unless, of course, there was some kind of catastrophic Incident.

5. Fold the diaper. Cloth diapers are usually cleaned and folded by a diaper service, but if you don't have a prefolded cloth diaper, you'll have to do it yourself.

- Lay the diaper out flat.

- Fold the eastern edge over one-third the width of the diaper.

- Do the same to the western edge.

- Now you have a long rectangle: Pull the top corners out a bit so that the rectangle is wider at one end. This becomes the end that gets pinned, once you've got a baby to pin it around.

6. Get the baby situated on a changing table or anyplace that's safe, warm, and soft. It's smart to lay a soft towel or changing cloth over the changing table—babies definitely do not dig cold, hard surfaces. As you go through the following steps, make sure to keep one hand on the baby at all times. They wiggle. You don't want yours to wiggle off the table.

7. Undo the diaper, making sure to keep the fasteners or pins out of the baby's reach. It's a good idea to put two fingers into the top band of the diaper as you undo the diaper pins, so that if the pin slips the wrong way it will poke you and not the baby.

8. If it's a boy, put a cloth diaper or something similarly absorbent over His Sprayness, because something about exposing it to the air tempts a baby boy to become a little pee fountain. And yes, he's aiming for your face.

9. Deal with the deed. If it's number one:

- Liquid is fairly easy to deal with. Fold the diaper over so that the baby's lying on the clean outside of the diaper.

- Proceed to step 10.

If it's number two, hold your breath and get in there:

- Lift the baby's feet with one hand.

- With the other hand, gently wipe off as much as you can with the diaper itself. Use the inside front of the diaper and wipe front to back. This is especially important for little girls, since wiping back to front can lead to infections.

- Fold the diaper over so the baby is lying on the clean outside of the diaper.

10. Clean up. Lift the baby's feet with one hand, and with the other, use a baby wipe (or two, or three, or four, depending on the size of the job) to wipe all the little folds and parts clean. Again, wipe front to back. Make sure you're thorough; if it was number two, lift the baby's feet and ankles up extra high for a second to check underneath.

11. Make a deposit. If you're dealing with disposable diapers, now's the time to pull the folded-over diaper out from under the baby, tuck the soiled wipes into the diaper, and if possible, reseal the diaper's adhesives. Now you have a neat package for the trash that contains most of the odor. If you're using cloth diapers, put the soiled wipes in the trash, pull the folded-over diaper out from under the baby, and set it aside for now.

12. Pat the baby dry. Use a clean, soft cloth or towel. Remember to replace the cloth over the mini-fountain if you're dealing with a boy—they especially enjoy a sneak attack just when you think the danger's almost over.

13. Apply a layer of baby powder, if that's what this baby's accustomed to—ask the parents. Tempting as it may be, don't just squeeze a big puff of powder onto the child's butt. In fact, don't squeeze the powder container at all— shake out half a handful (or up to a full handful for an older, larger baby), and pat the powder gently onto the baby's rump, thighs, and legs.

14. Slide a fresh diaper under the baby. Only one half of the diaper goes completely under the baby's bottom:

- If you're using disposable diapers, the end with the tape is the end that goes under the baby.

- If you're using cloth diapers, the end that you made slightly wider goes under the baby.

15. Fold the diaper up over the baby. If it's a boy, remove the spray-prevention cloth and make sure the mini-fountain is pointing down—so that when the fountain gets to work inside the diaper, nothing flows up over the waistband. Also, make sure that the diaper isn't bunched up between the baby's legs; the sensation is akin to the worst wedgie ever, and can cause skin irritation.

16. Fasten the ends.

If you're using disposable diapers:

- Remove the adhesive backing from the tape on one side, making sure not to let the tape touch the baby's skin.

- Pull the adhesive strip in and over to fasten it to the front of the diaper—it should be snug, but not tight.

- Do the same on the other side. When you're finished, you should be able to slide one finger into the waistband and feel the diaper tight around it.

If you're using cloth diapers:

- Fold the longer flap over the front of the diaper.

- Unfasten the safety pin or fastener.

- Insert a finger under the spot where the fabric overlaps, so you can keep the pin away from the baby. Use your thumb to hold the cloth tightly together.

- Pin or fasten the cloth so that it lays flat against your fingers.

- Do the same on the other side, making sure the diaper is one-finger snug.

17. Smooch. Lean over and kiss the kid on the forehead for not peeing in your face, or on your hands. Or worse.

18. If you're using cloth diapers and the job in question was number one, fold the diaper up into a tight ball and put it in the diaper pail. If it was number two, either hand the baby to someone else for a moment, or pick the child up and take him or her with you to the nearest toilet. Dump the contents of the diaper into the toilet. Show the baby the toilet and tell him or her that one day they'll understand what it's all about. Demonstrate the fun flushing mechanism. You're doing the parents a favor by sparking some early interest in toilet training. Do not drop the baby. When you're finished, put the soiled diaper in the diaper pail.

Troubleshooting

The baby doesn't seem to like this whole diaper-changing thing. Your job is a lot easier if you can somehow distract or entertain the baby so it won't notice that its pants are missing. Some ideas:

- Make up a song. Many funny ideas for songs will probably spring to mind.

- Give the baby a (water-repellent or easily washed) toy to play with.

- Keep eye contact. Make faces. Grin. Smile. Laugh. Babies are pretty suggestible. If this seems like fun to you, it'll seem like fun to the baby.

• Look closely for signs of redness and irritation: All that screaming and crying could be for a good reason. If you see diaper rash, tell the parents and be very very gentle as you wipe and dry the baby. Soothing ointments can be carefully applied with the fingers to help fight the irritation—ask the parents if they have some.

• Is there a fascinating mobile hanging over the changing table? Switch it on and let it run for a minute before you do anything else, or give it a suggestive tap to start the mesmerizing, fascinating, floaty movements. Babies love mobiles. Who doesn't?

• If there's no mobile, become one yourself. Make swoopy noises and move your head around slowly and strangely and fascinatingly while keeping eye contact. (Pause for anything involving pins or tape, though.) This behavior is usually sufficiently bizarre to intrigue fussy babies on the changing table.

If all else fails, power through and get it all done as safely and efficiently as you can. The baby may cry, but he or she just doesn't understand that you're trying to help.

Skills That Make the
World a Better, More Harmonious
and Decent Place

27.

How to Keep a Plant Alive for More Than a Year

Why You Should Learn This

People who have never been taught how to care for plants often call themselves, with a thin, defensive little chortle, "black thumbs." Never mind the fact that most civilizations are founded on the principle of trying one's best not to kill things. A good rule of thumb, whether yours is black or not: If you have killed something, try not to pass it off as cute, endearingly pathological carelessness. Own up to your mistake and try to do better.

Plants are living things. Plants make your house look good. Plants can suffer. You should try not to make them suffer. But please don't avoid houseplants altogether out of anxiety. Plants are the single easiest way to make your house homey and at-tractive—easier than painting the walls, easier than feng shui, easier than a new couch, easier than a dog. They add green life and graceful movement to a room—it's lovely to watch a frondy plant sway in the breeze from an open window. They can be sexy too: Try making your bedroom a bit of a love nest by draping a strand of lights over a willing ficus.

Like babies and pets, plants bring out the best in cohabit-ing couples. Helping something living to flourish is a subtle psychological thrill—although you don't necessarily need to take it that far. Just keep a plant alive for more than a year. You'll feel rewarded knowing you are all that stands between life and death for another living thing, and to it, you are a hero.

How To

Start Thinking of Houseplants as Born with Certain Inalienable Rights

Which are: water, food, sunshine, and a reasonable amount of self-determination. You are the benevolent dictator, the plant is your earnestly striving subject, which you treat with con-descending affection. Or if you prefer, you are the aunt or uncle and your plant is a precocious youngster: It needs your encouragement and care, but is ultimately not your most im-portant responsibility.

Find a Nice Place in Your House Where a Plant Could Live

Keep the Plant Rights in mind. That doesn't mean a table in the hall that you think would look nice with a plant. That means someplace a plant would be happy, which usually involves a window. The direction your window is facing determines the quality of the light, which in turn determines what kinds of plants will gladly grow there. If the window you want your plant to call home faces west or east, you need a plant that can take a lot of light and heat. Western windows in particular are hot, and can dry up plant soil—think cactus—but eastern windows are cooler with similar amounts of sun exposure, and flowering plants like African violets and begonias seem to dig them. If you have a northern-facing window, you should find a plant that doesn't need much sunshine: leafy plants (as opposed to flowering plants) tend to like northern windows.

Don't put plants next to anything that you yourself wouldn't like sitting next to for any lengthy amount of time: a heating vent, an air conditioner, a cold window pane, a draft, a radiator, a litter box, a two-year-old.

Find an Easy-to-Grow Plant that's Suitable to the Light and Space You've Got

It's always a good idea to buy your plants at an actual garden store because then you can ask questions and get advice from the salespeople. Here are some low-maintenance plants with excellent indoor track records:

• Cacti: Bristly, manly plants. You can also put nice-looking pebbles into their pots. Psychologically speaking, cacti are great kitchen and living room plants, and bad, bad, bad bedroom plants.

• Snake plants: These help create a secretive, whispery atmosphere, and come in beautiful shades of mottled green.

• Peace lilies: Real lord-of-the-jungle plants—shiny and smooth green. Can grow satisfyingly large.

• Philodendrons: Leafy, enthusiastic, and almost impossible to kill. These do well in north-facing windows.

• Begonias: It's hard to go wrong with these; they're some of the least fussy flowering plants around.

For advanced beginners

• African violets: These plants are so adorable and fuzzy and cuddly it's no wonder they're so popular, but they're harder than they look. Someone once told me, "No one under forty-five can make an African violet bloom." If that appeals to your competitive spirit, get an African violet. They do well if you keep a few simple rules in mind: Keep a paper towel under the pot in a dish, and moisten it so that water seeps up into the bottom of the container (change the paper towel often, or it will become unpleasant to look at and you won't like the plant as much). Never let water touch the leaves. And use high-phosphorous plant food to keep it in flower.

• Ficus plants: It's tempting to bring a mini-tree into your house, but what looks beautiful and lush in the plant store often looks desiccated and thin six months later in your house. Ficus plants are creatures of habit and drop their leaves at the first sign of trouble: Any difference in moisture, light, or fertilizer will freak it out completely. If you can provide a consistent supply of light and a scheduled supply of water and food, your ficus plant will calm down eventually and stop dropping leaves.

Feed and Water Your Plants

Do not forget. It's really not that difficult to remember—surely there are other things you do on a regular basis, like wash dishes or clean the house or take birth control or whatever. Combine the watering of the plants with a regular thing you do once a week: "It's trash and plants night" or "It's sex and plants night." Here's another way to remind yourself. Get a piece of paper and trace the picture on page 284. Color it pale green. Put it on your refrigerator door. If you're not artistically inclined you can also put a dried brown leaf some-

place prominent: on the fridge, on your desk, under your pillow . . . The point is to make plain to the part of your brain that tends to forget things that you are single-handedly responsible for something's life and it will suffer most horribly unless you take care of it.

Plants like big, long, infrequent gulps of water better than short, tiny, once-a-day sips. They also like room-temperature water better than cold, and if you can let the water stand out overnight so some of the ugly little tap water value-adds, like chlorine, have a chance to settle and/or evaporate, that's even better.

Plants are usually sold with a certain amount of nutrients already in the soil, and it takes some time for the plant to use all of these up. But you should start your plants on a regular diet of plant food as soon as you can anyway. Plant food usually has three things in it: phosphorous, which feeds the flowery part; nitrogen, for strong healthy leaves; and potassium, for sturdy roots. So pick your plant food according to what kind of plants you have: Ferns need more nitrogen; begonias need more phosphorous. In general, plants like being fed every other week, and you can start your plant on about half as much plant food as the package will tell you to use. Weirdly enough, most plants don't grow much during the winter months, even though they're inside and technically could grow year-round. So during the winter, feed your plant less, if at all, because it won't be using as much soil power.

Make Changes Gradually

Plants, like humans, fear change, and tend to be stunned for a few weeks after a big event, like all of a sudden getting more plant food or getting a new pot or being put somewhere else. Some plants are drama queens and may actually die if you shock them too much. So be tender. Be sensitive. Don't just move your plant to another room one day or start it on a high-nitrogen regimen because it looks a bit cross-eyed.

Keep the Air Around the Plant
Reasonably Full of Moisture

Most of the plants we consider houseplants are actually from the tropics. They like humidity, and most houses and offices aren't very humid. Misting isn't really the solution, despite what you may have heard—it's embarrassing for both you and the plant, and the water just evaporates right away anyway. A cool way to solve the humidity problem is to fill a pretty little shallow dish with water and pebbles and place it near your plant (or under it—but make sure the plant's bottom is not actually in the water). The water evaporates slowly off the rocks—much more slowly than it will off the plant's leaves— and provides a little more moisture in the air around your plant. A slightly less cool way to solve the humidity problem is to use a humidifier, if you don't mind explaining what it's for.

Be Supportive

You don't need to talk to to your plant if it makes you feel dumb. But an occasional encouraging whisper like, "Keep up the good work, buddy!" can't hurt.

Troubleshooting

My plant has little bugs and/or moldy spots on it. I want to throw it away. Don't! If you rub the leaves with water in the sink, or spray them with water, it usually helps. As a last resort, use pesticide, but apply as little as possible—it may take longer to solve the problem or infestation, but it's a small price to pay for having fewer toxins in the world and a healthy plant.

My plant has weird white crusty stuff on the dirt. That's residue from food it couldn't use. Cut back on the plant food.

My plant is droopy. You may be watering it too little or feeding it too much.

My plant leaves have brown tips. This is "tip burn," usually the result of chemicals in the plant's water. Cut back on the plant food a bit and try letting your plant water sit out overnight—there's about four times as much chlorine and fluoride in your average glass of tap water than a plant can really handle.

28.

———————————

How to Make Dogs and Cats Love You

Why You Should Learn This

It's not enough to seek the approbation and love of human-kind. We also want animals to love us, because they're furry and soft and interesting. You've probably known someone animals inexplicably cannot resist—the shy dog follows him adoringly, the grumpy cat always jumps into her lap—and that person, you have probably noticed, isn't necessarily ob-sequious or undignified around animals; he or she doesn't even need to try that hard. Animals can smell a phony the same as the rest of us. Note the admiration and surprise in the voice of the grumpy cat's owner when she says, "Wow, she really likes you!" Who wouldn't want that said about them?

How To

So what is it about that person? What makes him or her so attractive to animals? On some level, that person knows three things:

1. How to approach a dog or cat

2. How not to freak them out

3. What dogs and cats really like

How to Approach a Dog or Cat

As you are no doubt already aware, the two most common house pets have very different ways of interacting with the world. Lots of people believe in dividing the world into "dog people" and "cat people," although personally I'm not a big fan of that distinction—all dogs and cats just want love and care, smooches and kibbles, and it's no kind of world in which they don't get both. That said, given what we know about the evolution of dogs and cats, the difference in worldview between dogs and cats roughly translates into extrovert versus introvert, or *love me* versus *love me when I want you to and I'll make it worth your while.*

Dogs, given their own way, travel in packs; they're social animals. In a dog pack, there's usually a leader, or alpha dog, a couple of lieutenants to keep the alpha dog on his toes, a big pack of normal dogs, and an unfortunate crew of nerd dogs who hang around on the periphery, taking advantage of safety in numbers while trying not to be noticed and picked on. Dogs are constantly negotiating their own place on the social ladder, and for them, the two most important instinctual questions are pretty much, "Who is dominant?" and "Who likes me?" The sociology of dogs is a lot like high school, which may explain why human beings feel so supremely compassionate toward them—imagine a world in which everyday life, forever, is high school. Yes, dogs deserve our love, understanding, and guidance. You are your dog's awesome tenth-grade English teacher. Your dog thinks you are the best; he wants to be you when he graduates. We owe it to dogs to live up to their high expectations, and to be as cool as they seem to think we are.

Cats, as you've seen on nature shows, are solitary hunter types, who spend most of their time staking out territory and exploring or defending it. If dogs are like high school, cats are like a really tough Ph.D. program—or if that sounds hierarchical, then cats are like the quiet little kids who just want to be left alone to mess with stuff (some loner kids grow up to be wise and gentle, some become sociopaths . . . just like cats). A cat's facial and body expressions aren't as identifiable or human as a dog's, but there's no denying that at some point back in time, cats chose us because they like us. They wouldn't have allowed themselves to be domesticated otherwise. Their most important instinctual questions seem to be, "What the hell is that?" and "Is it mine?" And maybe, "Should I bite it or not?" We don't have to live up to cats, we just have to do our own thing and let them do theirs.

For both cats and dogs, every social interaction is all about trust. So you should approach dogs and cats in such a way that makes you easily identifiable as trustworthy, not biteworthy. To do this, just keep in mind the animals' basic instinctual questions, which must be answered before the animal will know what to do with you. And in general, you definitely want anything with sharp teeth and claws to know what to do with you.

For Dogs

Remember, the big questions are, "Who is dominant?" and "Who likes me?" The answer to both these questions, of course, is you, but while you want the dog to know you like him, you don't want him to feel like you're trying to establish dominance. Challenging a dog's status right away will make him dislike and distrust you (again, just like in high school). Some actions that humans think are friendly, dogs may see as a challenge. Submissive dogs will be scared by challenging behavior; dominant dogs will be antagonized by it.

How to introduce yourself to a dog: Say hello in a friendly voice, and squat down sideways near the dog. Clap, whistle, or continue speaking to him in a friendly way to get his attention, and let the dog come to you. Unless he's been abused or is extremely shy of humans for some other reason, the dog will almost certainly come to you, because you've established that you like him (by your warm tone of voice) without expressing any challenge (by your nonthreatening body language), and dogs are social creatures. When the dog approaches, don't lean forward toward him (moving toward a dog who's approaching you is one of those things we think is friendly and they think is aggressive). Just wait until he's right next to you, panting and looking interested. Say hello again. Gently stroke or scratch his coat from front to back. If he stays still or gets closer, he likes you.

For Cats

Again, it's important to recall the primal questions for all cats, which are, "What the hell is that?" and "Is it mine?" As far as question number one goes, the best thing about cats is that they really want to know what you're all about, because that's their nature—they're explorers and hunters. They want to check you out as long as it's not putting them in danger. But you can't fake it with a cat. If the answer to, "What the hell is that?" is "Oh, it's that kind of person I don't like" (and for some cats, you may well be that kind of person, through no fault of your own), then too bad for you, you can't get friendly with that kitty. Some cats are just judgmental. But most cats respect mutual curiosity, and if you both seem to be attempting to answer the "who are you" question at the same time—that is, if you convey to the cat that you find her inner workings as intriguing as she finds yours—then you have a better chance of making friends with that cat. Cultivate a sense of curiosity about cats and they will be curious about you.

As far as "Is it mine?," the most convenient answer for both of you, or the conclusion you want the cat to come to, is "yes." The cat will lay claim to you or not depending on whether or not she likes you. When she lays claim to you, you get to pet her whenever you want, and in fact, she'll start petting you (rubbing her face on you to leave her scent), which is pretty gratifying.

How to introduce yourself to a cat: From a respectful distance, make eye contact and say hello. While you're looking at each other, the cat will start assessing you—feel free to assess her right back. Be cool. Be patient. Reach down to her level and stick out your index finger while she's checking you out. Speak in a friendly, encouraging voice. She will probably come and sniff your finger—most cats seem to be totally incapable of resisting index fingers. When she does, she may actually take a shine to you and rub her face against your finger: That means you're hers. Gently scratch her under the chin until she's relaxed. If she moves around presenting different areas of herself for you to pet, she likes you. Or at least, she likes what you do for her, which with some cats is all you can expect.

Don't Freak Them Out

All dogs and cats have individual personalities—some are more laid-back than others, some like people more than others. But there are certain things that all dogs and all cats really don't like.

What to avoid doing around a dog: making prolonged eye contact; picking up a dog by surprise, by the scruff or by the armpits; and bending over to reach for a dog. Bending over from a position of power may make a dog feel threatened or challenged, even though you're just trying to pet him. Likewise, dogs make prolonged eye contact for the express purpose of figuring out who's the top dog, and when you stare at a dog, that's what he'll think you're trying to do.

What to avoid doing around a cat: picking up a cat by surprise, by the scruff or by the armpits; picking up a cat you've never met before; speaking loudly; and making an idiot of yourself in an attempt to be ingratiating. Cats respond to friendly tones of voice, but they seem uncannily aware when someone's condescending.

What Dogs and Cats Really Like

Not surprisingly, given their evolutionary history, dogs and cats come down on opposite sides on almost everything. For instance, dogs like repetition, and stroking or petting them the same way for a long time will feel really good. Cats get bored or frustrated by repetition, which explains why, in the middle of what you think is a perfectly nice petting session with a cat, she'll suddenly start biting and scratching you. She doesn't hate you, you've just bored her. The best way to pet a cat is not to pet any one part for more than a minute or so—change it up, move the love around (head, ears, chin, back, head, ears, chin, back, etc.).

Dogs like	Cats like
being petted on the chest or belly	scratching people who pet them on the belly (it's a game they play: If she presents her belly to you, don't rub it if you don't want to get scratched)
socializing	private time
challenges they can win	challenges they can't quite win
mimicking hunting	actually hunting
chasing actual things: people, Frisbees, balls	chasing invisible enemies, usually late at night

hide-and-seek	hide: Give a cat a box or a bag and she's entertained for hours just sitting in it
roughhousing	worship

Dogs and cats both like

• exploring

• being petted behind the ears, or lightly on top of the base of the tail

• being supported by the rump and the shoulders if picked up

• being rewarded for good behavior

• people

29.

How to Help Someone Out of a Car (An Older or Ill Person, a Woman You're Trying to Impress, Your Mother)

Why You Should Learn This

In America right now, somebody's turning sixty-five about every ten seconds. As people get older, they get less limber and agile, cars seem to get smaller and lower, or bigger and higher up off the ground, and young people don't seem to notice that getting out of a car is rather hard for them. Your grand-parents may already need a bit of an assist in the driveway-arrival department, and depending on what generation your own parents are, by the time you're in your thirties, they may appreciate a helping hand as well. Even putting aside the question of respect for one's elders, offering to help *anyone* get out of a car when it might otherwise be difficult for them isn't just a question of chivalry—although God knows older people, ill people, and pregnant people are certainly deserving of whatever benefits can be derived from our society's limited chivalric code—it's a necessary courtesy, and you want to do it with respect for the person's independence, even as you give aid.

And on a strictly ornamental level, a man's offer to help his date (or his mother, or some other grande dame du jour) out of a car is a gallant, completely unnecessary gesture, akin to opening a door or pulling out a seat. To many guys it may seem old-fashioned and lame, but women generally like it *because* it's old-fashioned and lame.

How To

As you can imagine, there's a distinction between helping someone who actually needs it and making a gesture of help in order to impress. For the person who actually needs it, you'll use your whole body to help. The person who just needs to know how thoughtful you are can make do with one arm.

Helping an Older, Ill, Pregnant, or Otherwise Not-So-Bendy Person Out of a Car

Keep in mind as you do this that you'll need to go quite slowly, and you'll need to give the person instructions on how to move so you can work together. Read the steps carefully, and commit to memory what *both* of you have to do. When you're explaining how you need the person to move, speak calmly and normally. Remember, this person may need your help, but is a grown-up, and the whole thing may not be very comfortable for him or her.

1. Ask. It's polite to help, but it's politer to ask if help is needed first. Don't make a big deal out of it, just say, "Hang on a minute and I'll help you out on the other side, okay?" and let them object if they're going to object. If you don't know them well enough to be that familiar, simply ask, "Would you like a hand getting out of the car?"

2. Open his or her door.

3. Get into position. The best place for you to stand is right next to their seat, angled in slightly toward the car. Make sure you're not standing on ice or in snow and have a firm footing.

4. Bend slightly at the knees and extend your outside arm (meaning whichever arm is the farthest away from the car door) into the car, in front of the person. You can hold out your hand or your entire arm, depending on how much support is needed.

5. Ask the person to take your hand or, if they need more support, your forearm or elbow.

6. Ask the person to swing their legs out. This is easier for some people than others, because it involves some swiveling of the lower body. The person will use your arm or hand as a sort of handlebar to help pull themselves around, and your job here is to be as steady as possible. Hold your outside arm and wrist very stiff, and let them use your strength for resistance. You can brace yourself, if necessary, with your inside arm on the roof of the car, or by resting your outside, supporting arm on the dashboard if the car is smallish.

If swinging both legs out is too difficult, ask that the person lift the leg nearest the door out and over the door frame. If the person cannot do this alone, you may help by lifting and moving the legs yourself.

- Place your hands under the knee joints and gently lift them together.

- Ask the person to hold one of your upper arms for support.

- Carefully move the legs to the side.

At least one of his or her feet should be able to touch the ground outside the car. If you are inconsiderate enough to drive an SUV, you'll probably need to provide a wide block or step, or guide the person's feet to the step rail or running board on the undercarriage—not the steadiest perch for anybody, so make sure you're supporting the person at all times.

7. With the person holding on to your outside arm, reach your inside arm in to support the middle back, with your hand flat against his or her middle back, or if needed, with your arm completely around the back.

8. As he or she pushes out of the car seat, you help pull the person up. The person should hold on to your outside arm with his or her outside hand (the hand farthest from you), and push off the car seat or frame with his or her inside hand. Try not to pull out too much, or the person won't feel in control of the movement—rather, let them do the pushing out as you do most of the pulling up.

9. Help the person stand and get his or her balance.

If he or she was able to swing both legs around and out:

• Keep your hand on his or her middle back until the person has brought all of their weight onto their feet and is standing straight.

If he or she was able to bring one foot down outside the car:

• Keep your hand on his or her middle back until the person has brought most of their weight onto that foot.

• Allow the person to lean his or her body weight against you as he or she lifts the other leg out of the car and places it on the ground.

• Gently help shift the person's weight onto his or her own feet and make sure she or he feels steady before you let go.

If you had to help swing his or her legs out:

• The person probably won't be able to put body weight on his or her feet until he or she is almost completely off the seat. Allow the person to lean on you as you guide him or her up out of the car.

• Gently help shift the person's weight onto his or her own feet and make sure she or he feels steady before you let go.

Helping Your Date or Your Mother Out of a Car

1. Don't ask. Just do. As you open your car door (first) say, "I'll be right around to help (or "escort" if you feel fancy) you out," so she knows not to preempt you.

2. Hasten to open her door.

3. Get into position. The best place for you to stand is slightly behind her seat, facing forward, legs slightly apart.

4. Lean forward and extend your outside hand into the car with a grin.

5. At this point, she'll swivel her legs out of the car and take your arm or hand (strangely enough, for women this usually seems to be rather instinctual; she probably won't need to be asked). If she takes your arm, put your other hand over hers so that no one else need see how tightly she grips.

6. Now she'll begin to push herself up off the seat. With a firm, stiff arm, help ease her out by pulling slightly up and away as she stands.

7. As she rises out of the car, take a half step away so she has room to emerge.

8. Close her door behind her with a flourish and be gratified by the flush of color on her cheeks. She'll pretend this happens to her all the time. It doesn't. You sly dog.

30.

How to Write Superior Thank-You Notes

Why You Should Learn This

One of the easiest ways to make people love you like crazy is to start writing good thank-you notes at every tactful, reasonable opportunity. Thank-you notes have a unique power: Written well enough, they make the recipient feel excellent, like a good and valued person, *especially* if they don't even think what they did was a big deal. You could do a lot worse than to go through life looking for ways to make other people feel good about themselves.

If you're like most people you probably associate thank-yous with a) job interviews, and b) gift-intensive situations like getting married or having a kid. But if the first time you write a heartfelt nonprofessional thank-you note is when you're slogging through a pile of your wedding presents, you are not a very nice person.

You will have many opportunities to be grateful as you grow older and wiser, and you may as well start marking those moments with style.

How To

Know When the Situation Warrants an Honest-to-God Thank-You Note

Here's a tip: When in doubt for crying out loud write one. If you're even considering the appropriateness of a thank-you note at all, then writing that note is less trouble than its intended recipient has probably already gone to on your behalf.

With that basic axiom out of the way, here's the real deal. It is imperative that you write a thank-you note when:

- Somebody recommends you for a job, or any other application

- Somebody interviews you for a job

- You have been a guest in someone's home (overnight or longer)

- You have been a guest on someone's dime

- Somebody does something nice for you that was above and beyond the call of duty (sends you flowers just for being so darn cute, helps you jump start your car at 7 A.M.)

- You are over sixteen and somebody gives you a gift —even if the gift itself is a "thank-you gift"

You may be looking at that last rule a bit cockeyed, thinking, "Surely the CD my good buddy got me for my birthday doesn't deserve a full-on thank-you note! What am I, a dork?" Okay, yes, sometimes your buddy can get a hug or a grateful email, especially if a semiformal gesture like a thank-you note will just make him or her uncomfortable. But really, when you think about it, it's our buddies who deserve our thanks the most, because unlike our families, they're not obligated to do a damn thing for us. The point is: Be sure to acknowledge every gift, no matter how casual, in the spirit in which it was given, times five.

The thank-you-note-for-a-thank-you-gift rule can also seem counterintuitive and belabored, but there's an actual logic behind that too: Thank-you gifts are most often shipped or sent, rather than given in person, and a thank-you note at once acknowledges the gesture and reassures the initial thanker (them) that the first-thanked (you) actually got the gift. And even if the thank-you gift was given in person, round-two thanking is just plain good manners and therefore doesn't hurt anybody. If writing a round-two thank-you really seems too demented for words, then call the person and say thanks, you shouldn't have.

You score cool points for writing a thank-you note when:

• You are under sixteen and somebody gives you a gift

• Somebody gives you a gift and you're currently sleeping with him or her

• You had a particularly nice time with somebody and just want to tell them so

There are actually some times when thank-you notes don't quite suffice, and you should accompany your note with a gift of some kind. Some examples:

• You're a guest at a wedding

• You're a houseguest for a weekend or longer

• You're the beneficiary of a kind gesture that costs the gesturer over $100

• Somebody throws you a party at which you get gifts

Know That a Thank-You Note Means a Note

It means paper, pen, and postage. People love getting things in their mailbox. Especially nice, non-bill things like thank-you notes.

When you do sit down to write your thank-you note, it helps to thank yourself first for being nice enough to do this at all. Make thank-you-note writing as pleasant a task as you can for yourself: grab a beer and/or a cup of coffee, sit comfortably in a nice sunny corner, use a really great pen, put the game on in the background. Give yourself some good time and space to write your note and it won't be such a drag.

Decide What Paper Is Appropriate

This is an issue that's been made needlessly complicated by etiquette cronies. Professional thank-yous are always typed or computer-printed on nice paper, or on a piece of quality cardstock. Everybody else gets a handwritten card. You may find it helpful to go ahead and buy a box of blank or preprinted cards for this express purpose the next time you see some you like. Opportunities to use them—all of them —will arise, sooner than you think.

Write a Rough Draft on Scratch Paper

There is an easy way to write a superior thank-you note. Draw a line down the middle of a piece of paper. The left side of the page is where you will write four simple, adjective-free sentence fragments, the *four essential elements of any thank-you note,* which are as follows, in this order:

1. The reason you're writing the note: the gift, the interview, the surprise party, the good deed.

2. How much you appreciated it. "I appreciate your thoughtfulness" is a good all-purpose phrase, unless you're writing a professional thank-you note, in which case use "I appreciate your time."

3. How great the note recipient is for giving/doing/sending/throwing it, unless you are writing a business thank-you note, in which case skip to number four.

4. Thank you.

If you followed the directions, you should have something like this:

A personal thank-you note

1. The picture frame you sent as a housewarming gift

2. I appreciate your thoughtfulness

3. It was really nice of you to send a present

4. Thanks so much!

A business thank-you note

1. Our interview yesterday morning

2. I appreciate your time

3. . . .

4. Thank you

Now on the right side of the paper, you add the *four essential embellishments,* which correspond directly to the four essential elements you just wrote:

1. If you are writing a personal thank-you, write one adjective that describes what this person did for you or gave to you. Some suggestions: *lovely, wonderful, great, cool, amazing, beautiful, gorgeous, perfect, unusual. Perfect* is actually a great word for thank-you notes; who doesn't like to be told that what they did is not just nice but *perfect*? *Unusual* on the other hand can be construed as a euphemism for *weird* or *ugly,* unless you have a reputation for genuinely appreciating unusual things. If this is a business thank-you, try an adjective like *helpful, informative,* or *interesting.*

2. Write one sentence that describes the very best thing, to you, about the gift, interview, or good deed—in other words, *why* you appreciated it.

3. If this is a personal thank-you for a gift or good deed, this is where you get to be a little creative: describe either a) how you've used the gift since you received it (keep it clean, people), or b) a way in which the good deed or gift has made your life a little better. If you haven't or it hasn't, of course, you need to lie. For business thank-yous, the third embellishment is a specific reference to something in your conversation that you found particularly notable, interesting, or useful. In other words, a little bit of elegant bullshit.

4. The fourth embellishment is a personal sign-off, to the tune of: "I'll see you soon," "I hope you and your family are all doing well," "I'll talk to you next week," etc. If you are writing a thank-you for a job interview, the fourth embellishment is always simply: "I hope to hear from you soon."

So the right side of your scratch paper should now look something like this:

A personal thank-you note

1. wonderful

2. The picture frame is just the right color for our new living room.

3. Now that we've moved, it's nice to have a place to display pictures of people from home.

4. Hope you're all doing well!

A business thank-you

1. informative

2. I enjoyed learning more about the company and hearing more about the position.

3. I was particularly interested to learn about how recent developments in the paper industry have affected the company.

4. I hope to hear from you soon.

The next step (again, do this on scratch paper first) is to smush the two sides of the paper together into complete sentences, using the following templates as guidelines:

Personal thank-you note

Thank you for the <u>wonderful</u> <u>picture frame you sent as a house-</u>
      [embellishment #1]   [element #1]

<u>warming gift.</u> <u>I appreciate your thoughtfulness,</u> <u>and the picture</u>
      [element #2]   [embellishment #2]

<u>frame is just the right color for our new living room.</u> <u>It was really</u>
                                     [element #3]

<u>nice of you to send a present.</u> <u>Now that we've moved, it's nice to have</u>
                    [embellishment #3]

<u>a place to display pictures of people from home.</u> <u>Thanks so much!</u>
                             [element #4]

<u>Hope you're doing well!</u>
[embellishment #4]

                                 Love,
                                 Your name here

Business thank-you note

Thank you for <u>*our interview yesterday.*</u>   <u>*I appreciate your time.*</u>
        [element #1]   [element #2]

<u>*I enjoyed learning more about the company and hearing more about*</u>
[embellishment #2]

<u>*the position,*</u> <u>*and I was particularly interested to learn about how recent*</u>
              [embellishment #3]

<u>*developments in the paper industry have affected the company.*</u>

<u>*Thank you again,*</u>   <u>*and I hope to hear from you soon.*</u>
[element #4]   [embellishment #4]

                                Best wishes,
                                Your name here

Troubleshooting

A good thank-you note is: natural-sounding, sincere, written promptly (but even a late thank-you is better than none at all).

A good thank-you note is not: gushy, overwritten, long.

Don't worry about: repeating the words *thank you, nice, great,* or *appreciate.*

Worry about: too many exclamation points (two is really the max).

Remember that: A business thank-you is really a formality—its sole purpose is to confirm for the recipient that you are a) still alive, b) still interested in the job, and c) not ignorant enough to neglect to thank your interviewer for his or her time. Your job interview thank-you is nowhere near as important as your résumé or the interview itself, and in fact, your note will almost certainly be chucked in the trash the minute it's read—unlike your résumé, of course.

About the Author

Siobhan Adcock currently lives in Ithaca, New York, where she is an M.F. A. student at Cornell University. Before going back to school, she was a writer and editor in New York City. She's almost thirty and still can't drive a stick-shift. This is her first book.